THE MILLION DOLLAR SEED

HOW TO WRITE YOUR BOOK AND BUILD AN EMPIRE

THE INSIDER'S SECRETS TO CREATING WEALTH AND LIVING YOUR DREAM

STELLA TOGO

TOGO PUBLISHING MEDIA PRODUCTIONS
Los Angeles · New York · London

The intent of this book is to offer information of a general nature to help the reader attain insight on the concepts and systems developed by the author. All stories, accounts and otherwise are based on the author's personal experience and recollection of events. This includes acknowledgements of various people, companies and otherwise who are mentioned within the content for the sole purpose of sharing the author's personal accounts and interpretations.

Published by Togo Publishing and Media Productions

www.togoproductions.com

Printed in the United States of America

Book Cover and Interior Design by Aaron Flisik

Author Photography by Linda Joseph–Silver Moon Photography

Library of Congress Cataloging-in-Publication Data

Togo, Stella.

The Million Dollar Seed: How to Write Your Book and Build an Empire

Stella Togo— 1st Edition

ISBN-13:

978-0615791968 (Togo Publishing and Media Productions)

ISBN-10:

0615791964

FOREWORD

BY JOHN KREMER

We live in one of the most exciting times in the history of books. Not only are books that can change people's lives easier to write and publish, but distribution and marketing of these books is easier as well. This means that more books are actually landing in the hands of the people who really need them.

For those who know me, I have lived happily in the book world for more decades than I care to admit, and I have seen many people come and go throughout the years. I have had the honor of working with some great iconic authors. With my love for marketing books, I continue to inspire many other authors to pursue *their* bigger and better visions.

I am so happy to know Stella Togo and to have worked with some of her clients. *The Million Dollar Seed* is a breath of fresh air. Anyone who dreams of writing a book and making lots of money with it needs to own *The Million Dollar Seed*.

Stella's mega-accelerated approach to writing and marketing bulldozes through old paradigms and focuses on innovative systems that work! *The Million Dollar Seed* immediately catapults you into a whole new mindset that works—a mindset that shows you how to become a successful authorpreneur in less than a year, so you can create wealth and live your dream now.

John Kremer

Author of *1001 Ways to Market Your Books*
BookMarketingBestsellers.com
HugAnAuthor.com

DEDICATION

To my children, Christopher and Arianna—

May you always live earnestly and realize your dreams

ACKNOWLEDGEMENTS

I wish to acknowledge my team of truly incredible professionals that made it possible for me to get this work published in record time. Thank you for all of the expertise, time and personal care you dedicated to this project. I am forever grateful. I also wish to acknowledge those who have made an impact in my life and whom I hold dear to my heart.

Aaron Flisik—Thank you for designing a cover that is not only captivating but just like the words—strong in conviction. You did an excellent job in implementing that refined presence to the interior pages. You truly captured my vision and brought spectacular dimension to it!

William Shane Tucker—Thank you for editing this work and making it a priority within your busy schedule. As always, your expertise is superb. Your efficiency, quality of service and turnaround time was astounding!

Karen Schmedeke—Thank you for designing a fabulous logo brilliantly displaying a person with an open book that also looks like a magic lamp! Your talent simply amazes me.

To my dear friend, John Kremer—Many people have heard me refer to you as my personal Santa because working with you always brings me such astonishing gifts. Every day is like Christmas with you. Your assistance in helping me with the title for this book is a sheer example of your comprehensive expertise. I wholeheartedly appreciate your extraordinary knowledge. Thank you for the joy you bring to my life and to my clients.

Angelique Rewers—Thank you for being the match that ignited the passion behind this project when you invited me to speak at The Insider's Edge. Your leadership and dedication to corporations, business owners, and entrepreneurs are exceptionally respected! You are such an inspiration to me and to all who know you.

David Neagle—Thank you for being such a powerful mentor and coach. You have completely changed my life by expediting my attainment of insurmountable realizations. I feel so fortunate to know you and to be graced with your mastery.

The Neagle Team—Thank you to all of the coaches and individuals who support me with my business and personal growth. Every one of you is to be applauded for your tremendous assistance, genuine care and incomparable service.

Martha E. Bowers—Thank you for all of the many hats you wear in my life. Everyone should be so blessed to have a "Martha" in their life. Thank you for being my soul sister and business confidant. I am forever grateful for the love you poured with me into this work. Your loving support made it possible for me to bring this project to life in record time.

To my dear friend, Elle Keith—Thank you for all your love and support throughout the years. Your feedback and wonderful creativity always make it fun to call you on a pinch when I need to bounce something off of someone. I am so grateful to have you in my life. Thank you for being such a great friend.

June Futamase—Thank you for being there to witness and celebrate my personal and professional achievements with me throughout my life. Thank you for sharing your wisdom and for the laughter we share! I am so happy you are in my life.

Patricia Johnson—My heart is filled with tremendous gratitude every time I sit in my work space. Thank you for adding beauty and inspiration to my environment. You are such a gift to my life. I love you dearly for all the happiness you bring me.

Linda Joseph—Working with you was simply a blast! You really captured exactly what I needed with my photo. Your expertise helped me feel at ease and comfortable in front of the camera. Thank you for making it so fun and easy for me.

My Togo, Dicillo, and Dacchille Family in Italy—Although we are far apart, you are never far from my thoughts and my heart! Thank you for bringing the party every time we talk! Thank you for your love.

To all of my book writing and author clients—who have given me the privilege and opportunity to work with them—Thank you for the profound knowledge each of you has shared with me given your professional mastery and years of developed proficiency. I am simply awe-struck when I think of how much I've learned from each of you and all of the different genres.

I am intensely humbled by your extraordinary commitment toward changing people's lives. You are the ones who are actively making a difference. It moves me when I think about it—certainly you must know the world is a better place every time a child is acknowledged, a marriage is saved, a business soars, and a person is inspired! I thank you with all of my heart for your passion and leadership. Thank you for making my life so rich!

INTRODUCTION

Recently, I was asked to speak for a large group of business owners, entrepreneurs and professionals. I realized it was time for me to write and offer my audience a new book that could be of value to them in their business. It is noteworthy to mention this event is scheduled to take place in about four weeks from the time I am writing this introduction. I authored this body of work in about fifteen days—a far cry from the five years it took me to write my last book! Now, I don't suggest anyone do this alone in their home as they may risk losing their fingers in the process!

The inspiration for writing *The Million Dollar Seed* has been percolating for a while, and this invitation was the catalyst I needed to bring it to fruition. Needless to say, my excitement took over with a new sense of urgency.

I found myself amused by how fast the words appeared on the screen of my computer. Having a goal of being published as well as having books on hand for this event initially seemed both daunting and exciting for me. There's nothing like setting a goal that may seem impossible to attain, which allows me to really see what I'm made of!

Perhaps the greatest sense of gratification is merited in knowing that things come easily when you've mastered them. In order to achieve my objective, I made the decision to do what I coach and mentor others to do! Setting my designated plan took priority over nearly everything with the exception of serving my clients and taking care of my daily responsibilities.

As a side note, it is important to mention that I usually coach people to write their books within three to six months, along with helping them accelerate their business growth. In terms of writing and publishing there are dynamic strategies, disciplines and industry specific standards of which are all taken into consideration and require professional guidance. With the accelerated approach, the time allotted lends us outstanding efficiency toward establishing market credibility, brand extensions, an ideal platform and income opportunities.

Having a powerful built-in support team to handle each delicate component throughout the publication process is very significant. Managing each individual on my team was much like managing a relay race as each person had to be precisely accurate with their skills and timing or else it could have thrown the whole thing off course. As the leader of the team, I had to do my part in providing clear and concise directions to each person.

While giving my focus readers a chance to review

my writing as it was completed, I sent my editor what they sent me the day before! The cover was being designed while I approved the edits for each page. In the meantime, I created the content, received releases, testimonials, an endorsement and foreword–all while making a *ton* of decisions.

I happily worked around the clock quite literally as my editor is in London and my cover designer is in New York. Working from my home office made it easy to write at night and in between my coaching calls. Thank goodness for the Italian espresso because it sure helped me with my focus and drive to reach my desired outcome!

It is with tremendous passion, intention, and love that I share the content within this work. My experience of working with writers and authors for more than ten years has shown me that there is a real need for people to efficiently approach the idea of writing and marketing with a whole new mindset or perspective. The idea that becoming a financially successful author has to be hard and that it requires a lot of time to reach your financial goal are truly old paradigms.

In fact, most people will write their books and later look for those who will buy them. If you take anything at all away from this body of work, please adopt the information and immense importance of knowing your market preferably and ideally before writing your book.

With my earnest commitment to the financial realization of writers and authors, I share insights, experiences and systems demonstrating that one can easily reach their goals in a timely fashion. This new approach using proven methods and strategies will certainly accelerate the leap to success for almost anyone.

I increasingly see many people writing books without a monetary goal or desired outcome in place. My mind boggles when I think of why writers and authors typically leave the marketing aspect as their last priority. I can't tell you how often I speak with individuals whom have written a manuscript but have never really given thought as to whom might buy their published version. If I had a dime for every conversation like that, I would be a very wealthy woman!

When you think of the consumer market in regards to other professions and industries, things are usually made to be sold to people who need those products. We call them products because they are produced for the purpose of being sold to a mass market. So, why would the mindset of a writer or an author be any different? Isn't a book a product?

A car was not invented to just sit in a garage any more than a book, published or not, is written to just sit on a shelf! Think of what an injustice it would have been if Karl Benz, inventor of the first modern car in 1886, kept it hidden from anyone to experience! Yet how many books, published or otherwise, ever make it past the owner's desk drawer or book shelf?

You will see me refer to both writers and authors individually instead of lumping them together into one category. For me, there is a clear distinction between them. I refer to writers as those who are in the process of writing a book but not as of yet published authors. On the other hand, I refer to authors as those who have written and published their book or books. Although there are similar needs that cross over each category, I feel it is important to speak to both in order to respect each as a separate market with diverse objectives.

The writer is like a Karl Benz who creates or invents a concept while Henry Ford is like the authorpreneur who takes flight with that idea. Like Ford, the author develops assembly line techniques for mass production of products so as to help the largest number of people!

The knowledge and expertise I share within these pages is intentionally written to benefit the largest number of people within each of these categories. Having worn both hats myself, I can intimately speak to possessing a diversity of understandings and proficiencies. "The Ten Most Common Marketing Mistakes Made by Writers and Authors" is also included in this book to spotlight a topic that is so foreign to many writers and authors.

I have by design written *The Million Dollar Seed* as an example of what an industry specific, how-to book needs to contain within its content. I am purposely positioning it as a foundation for several other books, products and services. Every word, sentence, page, and chapter has been carefully thought out so it builds onto itself with meaning and conscious marketing intention. Each of the elements on the front and back covers has been given special attention in order to make it easier to attract those who need this information.

Regardless of where you are in your writing or marketing process, the accelerated systems I have established will naturally integrate within your scope of an empire mentality. One of the many tools I offer are "The 9 Steps to Plant Your Book as The Million Dollar Seed" before you write your book. These steps are designed as a fundamental structure or starting point that are also relevant to authors. They speak to the lifeline of having a strategic plan for boundless progression.

I use the word *empire* to take people beyond what they think is possible with their concept and business. I love to visit that place of curiosity with them. From there, we can create an array of projected products and/or services. It's just so much fun as the creative side of the writer or author gets to have permission to play!

Through my own personal accounts and the successes of my clients of whom I share, you will find the journeys that led us beyond what was initially thought possible! Every one of them was thoughtfully selected for each designated section. Each client, regardless of genre, brings their own individual fingerprint to make their mark for the betterment of humankind.

More than one client has referred to their experience as *magical.* What they didn't realize at first was the magic was within them. It was always there just waiting to be freed through the expression of their desires!

The *Million Dollar Seed* approach to writing and marketing your book takes on a life of its own with each person who embraces it as a possession. Like a beautiful waterfall it cascades into all other areas of one's life, making it richer and more gratifying in so many ways.

Throughout these pages you will find helpful questions and many marketing concepts that will guide you to what is possible. When we train ourselves to look for what is possible, countless opportunities suddenly have a way of finding us. It is simply a matter of preparing ourselves to receive those blessings so we can clearly see them.

I've also included "The Top 15 Streams of Income" to expand on several of the strategic points made for increasing your revenue. Creating a fully thought out product, knowing who needs it and knowing how to offer it to them is the key to building your empire.

I wholeheartedly celebrate your curiosity for what's possible as well as your scope of knowledge in every sense of the word. May you discover a whole new world within these pages and see how easy it can be to create wealth and live your dreams! What is the title of *your* million dollar seed and who will you plant it for?

TABLE OF CONTENTS

"Anything can be possible the minute you decide it is!"

-Stella Togo

CHAPTER 1

LIVE IN POSSIBILITY

I remember it as if it were yesterday: It was June 1992 and by far the most terrifying twenty-four hour period of my life as I waited for my doctor to call me with the results that catapulted me into a whole new world of profound possibilities. Being 32 at the time, it all seemed hard to wrap my head around what might happen! My restless mind tearfully took me to all the dark places thinking that if it *was* cancer, I could die and not be there for my beautiful babies.

Yet, what happened next was beyond anything I could've ever imagined! When the call finally arrived and the answer was 'yes', I began to feel every cell of my body renew with an unknown sense of strength and excitement for what I knew I needed to do to live! Perhaps it was the seven months prior of daily meditations or the mother in me that began to visualize watching my children grow up to be amazing people that aligned me with a keen knowing that I *would* overcome breast cancer. That day was over twenty years ago and it was the catalyst for how I have lived my life since: with gratitude, staying focused on my desires and dreams while continually exploring other worlds of possibilities for me, and all who are interested in experiencing more life.

It was just a few months after my diagnosis that I began my arduous five year writing journey that led me to first self-publish *In Honor of Women: A Revolutionary Approach to Preventing Breast Cancer*. There were three constants that resided in my mind throughout those five years. The first was to do everything necessary to live in the mindset of possibility and never settle for *anything* less, along with the focus of raising my children. The second was to shed light on the topic of breast cancer with my book and the third constant was my big dream of selling my rights to a large house—all of which fed my desire for more life!

With the delivery of every one of my sixty letters plus of rejection from editors and publishers, I grew more passionate to get my work into the right hands. It seemed the more no's I received, the deeper I delved into staying focused on my desire, no matter how painful it was to go to that mailbox!

Had it not been for the women who wanted

to learn more about my book, and who ultimately became part of my personal study, I would have never written the third and final version of my book. My curiosity got the best of me, as I longed from my own diagnosis to know why women thought they got this disease. I so desperately wanted to know what women thought and why the disease showed up in epidemic proportion.

To my advantage, I discovered that writing a book was much like being pregnant because everyone asked, "How's the book coming along?" As more breast cancer survivors started coming out of the woodwork, I started to ask them questions that led to my discoveries of the ten emotional and psychological commonalities directly linked to breast cancer.

Since my prior how-to and autobiography drafts weren't working for the publishers, I thought these findings would surely spark some interest in them. So for twelve weeks I wrote from 9 pm at night, in the quiet while my children slept, until 6 am the next morning. I'd wake them up to be part of their morning and wish their little hearts a great day before my husband at the time would take them to school. I then would go to sleep until 1 pm and start my day. I remember thinking that it would all be worth it if I could just show one woman the psychology of this disease and how to prevent it.

I promised myself that if I ever got picked up by a well-known publisher, I would help make writing and publishing so much easier for others. I just knew there had to be an easier way than how I did it! Not having a degree in journalism, and English being second to my Italian language certainly didn't enhance confidence.

I can't tell you how many people attempted to discourage me from continuing my efforts—how many times people asked why I'd put myself through so much rejection especially after all my surgeries, recovery, *blah, blah, blah!* After all I wasn't even a doctor, so who would buy my book?!

Ironically, I learned that many of those whom I called friends soon fell off my list. My new found mindset of both what I needed to do in order to break free of my emotional cancer and what I needed to do to achieve my dream as a published author had no tolerance for them.

They were the same folks who thought I was in denial when I told them I was having champagne and gourmet lunches to celebrate life with the father of my children while receiving chemotherapy. Their response was, "Well, what do the doctors have to say about that?"

What most people didn't understand was that I wouldn't be alive if I had listened to what some doctors had said to me. I learned pretty quickly that it didn't matter if the outside world failed to understand me or what I was doing! I simply had to separate myself from those individuals and their fears, which they perhaps unknowingly were so willing to project onto me. I had to stay focused and listen intensely to the voice within to guide me.

Whenever my own doubts and fears regarding my writing haunted me, I knew the stories of my fellow survivors would ultimately carry much more weight than any self-doubt standing in my way! I often say, "We write the books that teach us the most!"

I received a call from Random House three months after I self-published my work. This call was the one I had been waiting five years for! Within minutes I called one of the most reputable agents in New York City who responded to me five minutes after I left her a voice mail message. Now, mind you she didn't know me, and I had not spoken with her until then.

Within days, she had me in front of countless major publishers in the city. I thought my feet were going to fall off as we walked from one big publishing house to another in those three very hot and intensely humid, summer days. It didn't matter that my silk suit was sticking to me nor that I couldn't feel my feet anymore. Sitting where some of the greatest writers had sat with some of the finest authorities in the publishing world made it seem surreal and yet so worthwhile!

My agent soon created a bidding war, and within two days we reached an amazing agreement in collaboration with Ballantine Books—a division of Random House—who published my second edition in May 1998. They graciously gave me a contract, a wonderful advance and provided me with a ten-city, seven day, West Coast book tour. When I asked the vice presidents at Ballantine Books what changed their minds since they had just rejected the same manuscript three months prior, their response was that they absolutely loved my cover design.

They then stated what surprised them most was seeing Marianne Williamson's endorsement on my cover as well as four other bestselling author endorsements on the back. I explained that it had taken me a year after meeting Marianne in LA to get her endorsement in Cairo, Egypt. I realized after the conversation my desire for attaining my goal as a traditionally published author was so strong that perseverance and determination had become a natural way of my being.

I loved my editor and her team. I remember crossing one of the busiest streets in New York City with her and my agent on our way to lunch. While stepping onto the street, she placed her right arm in front of me to protect me. She looked at me and said,

"We can't let anything happen to our author!" I remember smiling at her in gratitude for the acknowledgement.

Little did I know my desire to assist writers in becoming successful authors would later position me as a book writing and marketing acceleration coach. Shortly after my tour and continued launches, I started looking at ways to take writers through a process that would be most efficient and easy for them. I knew if I was going to remain true to the promise to myself, I would need to find a way for writers to get their books done in a much shorter time frame than my five years.

I thought of how painful it had been to relive and rewrite all of my emotional sections, in addition to all the time it took me. Personally, I wouldn't wish that on anyone! I didn't feel I could really serve anyone if I couldn't save them time and lots of frustration. I thought of how wonderful it would be to help someone else recount their story without ever having to relive their painful experiences again.

I kept wondering, "Is it possible to really write a book once without *any* drafts? What would I need to do in order to avoid rewriting a book several times, and how do I get to the end result quicker?… *and* if I could do it in less time, how soon could I get it published?"

As I played with the idea, it occurred to me to start from the end result! With a solid structural basis, I developed a system and format that allowed writers to effectively embrace the idea of writing their book only one time. This was such a huge epiphany for me as I realized it was no longer a possibility but a definite reality! Once I recognized I could take a writer through the process in three to six months, I then began to identify how to handle their needs based on their skillset and vision.

My focus was immediately placed on their passion and on a variety of possibilities to make their process both enjoyable and practically effortless. It was important to acknowledge while most experts usually had their knowledge readily available, a book could write itself with the right guidance and organization. Not only was it possible to write a book without writing several drafts, it was now down to a science. As my client Steve Schloss would say, "Yeah! Baby!"

First Things First: The Concept or Idea Behind Your Million Dollar Seed

One of the key factors to identify first and foremost is the concept behind the book that you want to write and share with the masses. Is this a concept that can lead to other products, such as a series of books for different markets? Is this a concept that allows you to show your brilliance with your skillset, such as a speaker or a blog talk radio host? What are some of the possibilities that can be created or developed in terms of other products and services?

Be it a novel, a guide, a how-to, a children's story or an industry specific business solutions-based book, it matters not what the genre or type of book it is. It is vital to know what the concept behind *your million dollar seed* is so we can breathe life into it!

My approach with each and every client has been to bring forth *the fingerprint* of that individual in order to harness their particular expertise, and in doing so, we completely avoid competition. In fact, competition doesn't even exist in my world because no two people take the same approach based on their unique and personal background or information. I do, however, also recommend to my authors and writers to avoid reading other works related to their own while writing for obvious reasons.

There is no greater time than to look at the possibilities of what can be created or developed before a book is written or published! Though many writers come to me after they have written and even published their work, it is never too late to explore the possibilities that are available. When it comes to the development of a particular concept behind a book, the sky is the limit!

I am always interested in learning about a

writer's vision and curious to see if that vision can be expanded into something bigger. People often think way too small simply because no one has ever showed them a different way or mindset. Let's face it: the days of selling one book at a time are nearly extinct, especially given recent technological advances.

Depending on your dream or desire, your vision can grow as big as your willingness to achieve it. But before we go to the vision, we need to fully embrace the idea or concept; in addition to all of the fullness and meaning it carries for you as the writer.

By starting with the end result in mind, we look at how big we can grow the concept first! A concept is as simple as an idea, perception, thought or conception. What is it about that idea that intrigues you the most?

The *WHY* Behind the Concept or Idea for Your Book

So often understanding the passion or what drives the concept within a writer helps me better understand the positioning of the work and how we can expand upon it with other products, services and programs. We look at the *why* behind the concept to give it depth and full meaning for the writer and their respective audiences. Understanding this aspect with the writer gives us clarity on some of the angles that can be taken from a marketing and branding standpoint.

I believe it is important to really look at your *why* and see how deep it runs in your core or passion. Here are three questions to ask yourself. These questions are postured for you to gain some clarity on your purpose and significance for what drives you to write your book.

> *Why do I want to write my book?* Be very specific here if you can! Though many will say to help people, there is usually a more defined meaning behind their reason. For example, would it help you somehow by giving you credibility in your industry or business? Did you experience or overcome something that you could shed light upon? Getting clear on all that lives behind the *why* is most helpful as it will add depth for you and your project.
>
> *What would happen if I never got a chance to share my concept or if I couldn't sell my book due to lack of marketing strategies?* If you would feel devastated, sad or deeply disappointed, then this tells you your passion and desire will carry you through the process.
>
> *How would I feel if I never got to write my book or get published?* If you're response is,

"Life will go on!" then that tells you you're either not committed to the idea of writing your book or you may not be ready just yet, which is perfectly alright. But if it makes you feel miserable just at the thought, well then, I'm thrilled for you!

The answers to these questions are what will drive you based on their importance and built-in sense of priority within your core.

I love it when people come to me with an indescribable, burning desire to write a book. They've thought about it in some case for years, and they just have to bring out what has been lying dormant within them for a long time—in some cases decades. Usually it's the type of person that is burning inside who will more than likely make a mark and impact the world in a very positive way.

A few years ago, I met a woman who said she started writing her book more than sixty years ago! I was awestruck and momentarily at a loss for words! Here I thought my five years was quite the task, but sixty years made my five look like a walk in the park! Bless her heart, she was ninety-five and had quite the story to tell! Unfortunately, she passed before we really got a chance to work together.

I think about her sometimes and wonder how her life may have been different if she had found someone to help her with her book way before I came along. Although she lived a very full life, I know from her excitement that she would have loved to share her story.

The individual who is more than driven to share their concept, idea or story is usually whole-heartedly determined and vastly believes in it. In many cases, the concept or idea is based on a very personal experience. My own experience shows me that nothing would have stopped me from writing my book, especially once I started gathering data from the other cancer survivors.

I deeply wanted to share my discoveries, as so many of the answers to the questions in my study were practically verbatim. The project became bigger than me as I wanted to help other women understand that breast cancer has a profound message, and that it doesn't for the most part just happen for the heck of it!

Though it is at times hard to admit, there are many reasons that can stop us from completing our work. It is easy to find excuses that can prevent us from moving forward when the mind wants to keep us playing safe and small. I've not only heard these kinds of messages in my own head but a million times over with clients. Mind chatter like, "I don't think I can write well" or "who would buy my book?" or "what if I write the book and no one buys it!"

What's interesting though is that when we fully understand the depth of our *why* behind the concept of writing a book, we won't easily be swayed by those thoughts because it is in our intrinsic nature to really want to help others.

Oddly enough, the people who don't think that they can write often are the ones who write profoundly from the heart—moving me and their readers to tears. It is generally the person who feels they may not be good enough who offers the very message the world needs to receive in order for others to be inspired! Imagine the possibilities of what that one voice and one thought can do for our consciousness! I have seen incredible examples of this with many people whom I've had the privilege and honor of working with: some of whom I share within the heart of these pages.

In my experience of working with writers and authors, I can feel the pulse of the growing number of people who want to make a difference with their ideas and stories. I will say that there has never been more of a need for people in recent years to write their books and to use their *why* for the sheer sake of making it easier for the next person. Isn't that why we build communities to support each other in a variety of different ways? Why we create non-profits, go into business, choose new careers, etc.?

It is all about helping each other live the best

life we can live while overcoming obstacles no matter how big or small! Right? Think of the books that have made a difference in your life. How wonderful is it when we can enhance our human experience with and for each other?

So, when you look at a concept or idea for writing *your million dollar seed*, you want to look at the impact it can potentially make with your particular skill set. We want to dig as deep as you are willing in order to identify what you consider to be your strengths! Here is where we want to go the extra mile so no stone is uncovered or missed; this means that at times people can undoubtedly overlook or take for granted the very things that come easy for them! I take it upon myself to help individuals identify those things that need to be uncovered as strengths so we can potentially include them within their platform.

Working with Steve Daguio, author of *Make the Play of Your Life,* was truly exceptional because his life's work was based on helping young athletes get scholarships in divisions ll, lll and NAIA Universities and colleges so they could play the sports of their dreams. His personal stories including what happened to him and both his sons, as well as other young athletes he helped for more than two decades, show his dedication to his message in his book.

Now, what was interesting is that he was never paid for his time or services. As he wrote and self-published his work, he began to see the value of what he could offer as an author, speaker and coach. It was easy to see that speaking and coaching had been practically effortless for him since he had been one for years. These were two very important skills that would be instrumental in building his platform and business with his book. As it turns out, he is truly brilliant as a speaker with lots of expertise in his field. Listening to him speak is such a joy! He has such a way of drawing his audience in and completely captivating them.

For many, the *gems* are already there when it comes to bringing out the brilliance within the writer and the person. I refer to *gems* as skills that literally become activated once the *why* is given voice. It is so exciting for many clients to harness what has been residing within them for many years. You see when the *why* is so strong within a person, not only is it easy to identify those *gems*, but it is virtually impossible to derail them as they have to complete their book.

One of the most amazing things about Steve is that when it came to writing his book, his passion and drive was beyond comprehension. What most people don't know about him is that he had to overcome some very major obstacles that could have easily stopped him from writing his book. I mean the kind of things he experienced would normally break someone at the knees. Instead, he kept moving forward without a glitch.

I remember the day he called to tell me his house had partially burned down. He along with his family had to move to a hotel until his home could be rebuilt! A few months later, I received another call from him notifying me he had been in a serious car accident: t-boned at an intersection by someone who flew through a red light at sixty miles per hour. The fact that he is alive is truly a miracle!

The Skillset that Builds a Platform

One of the greatest myths that haunt most writers and authors today is that they have to have many skills. It is really a matter of identifying what skills fit their particular vision. People tend to get in their own way because they feel they have to be great writers, great speakers, great thought leaders, etc. In actuality, all we need to remember is to be efficient and great in what we offer in order to get paid well for it. That said, it is important to spend time and focus on doing the things you love and want to learn that can be added to your platform or skillset.

For example, if learning another language is a point of interest to you and you would like to branch out to another culture as part of your extended speaking platform and market revenue, then I would highly encourage you to do that! I actually know several people who have two separate cultural markets, and both markets have been very successful for them.

The point of exploring your skillset is to help you as an author, grow your market with your expertise so you can do more of what you love to do! Some people love the technical aspects of business, while others would much rather be out there in front of the crowds.

Obviously, teams are built to do the very things we don't love or want to do within our businesses. However, in order to live in possibility, it is important to think outside of the box while looking at where our passion lives in terms of a variety of facets for a particular platform. It's clear to see that there isn't a box or a peg that best fits everyone, given the individuality of a person and their preferences.

What works for one author may not work for another and not everyone wants the big enchilada of the empire. Maybe they want just a piece of it, and that is perfectly fine. In fact, some folks can't even see past being published and that's okay, too. There is no judgment. The most important aspect to remember is that significant thought should be placed into what you really want to achieve as a result of your efforts, before you embark on the goal of writing your book.

Here are some questions I like to ask writers and authors in order to get an initial sense as to what skills we can focus on so as to help them achieve their potential. Remember I am looking for what lights someone up.

What Lights You Up?

Do you love to teach, train or be in front of a group of people?

Do you love to work from home and stay on your computer all day creating, writing and promoting programs, connecting with other people online, etc.?

Do you love to create new products or programs before or after writing a book?

Do you love to research?

Do you love to manage people?

What are the parts of your concept that you love the most?

Do you love to collaborate with others or work on your own?

Are there areas within your skills that need improvement, perhaps where a particular coach could add enhancement?

What areas do you need help with?

What areas do you feel you are great at, can excel in and do more of?

I believe that fact-finding is an important aspect of this process. This kind of awareness and insight can save you time as you gain a clear understanding as to what is important to you.

Combining Vision and Concept with Endless Possibilities

"If you can see it, you can achieve it. God helps those who help themselves. Power is in the act of humility." Patricia Amis

I love this quote so much! It speaks beautifully to the essence and the desire of becoming a powerful author, to the willingness of a person who can step into what he or she needs to do, as well as to come from humility in truly serving those for whom we write or speak.

Let's look at this for a moment. When we can see or imagine ourselves living a dream, and we do what it takes to show up at every turn with authenticity, we then can feel humbled for the opportunity to share our message. One of the most profound moments I experienced as an author was after speaking for a large group of breast cancer survivors. I sat down at my table to sign books and was taken by the length of the line of people waiting for me. I can't tell you how many times I visualized myself sitting at a book signing long before my book was completely written!

I was so humbled as one by one, the women thanked me for coming out to speak and for writing the book. So many of them said, "I felt like you were speaking directly to me and that you were telling my story." Remember my first initial goal was that if I could reach one woman and share with her the psychology of breast cancer then it would all be worthwhile. Well my cup runneth over that day and many that followed with incredible gratitude for the opportunity to share my message with women everywhere.

Once we have identified the skillset of an individual and have a keen sense of their vision based on their idea, then we can begin to explore the contents of the book. As a result of my own writing experience, I developed a powerful exercise that allows the writer to beautifully bring forth their most fundamental points within an hour or less—and then we are off to the races! We then will take those key points and help structure the information, which then allows me to see what can be developed into a variety of future products, programs and services.

This is where the fun really begins! However, keep in mind that one of the main factors is that everything is identified, discussed, organized, planned out and done in a very methodical way. Every piece, component or section of *a million dollar seed* as a first book needs to be positioned like a building block for growth and expansion in the near future. Building an empire with one book starts with living in the dream and possibility of what can be achieved!

Can you think big? REALLY BIG! I invite you to take a moment to answer these 7 questions for yourself before going to the next chapter. Do your best to be really honest with yourself and specific here. I would suggest using the *Million Dollar Seed* Notes section in the back of this book to write your answers.

The 7 Questions to Prepare Yourself for Writing *Your Million Dollar Seed*!

If I could do anything with my book, what would I like to do?

What are the possibilities around my success?

How would my life be better if I were a published author?

Who will benefit from my book?

What will they learn from my experiences that will improve their life?

What philanthropic or humanitarian achievement would help me feel more fulfilled?

What message do I want to shout out at the top of the tallest mountain?

"90% of your marketing is done once you know your market."

– John Kremer

CHAPTER 2

WRITE FOR YOUR MARKET

One of the most common mistakes I find writers and authors make quite frequently is that they don't take the time to really study their market before writing their book. This is by far *the* most important aspect in regards to being an author that merits your attention, especially before you lay the groundwork with your content. It can be much more challenging to address your marketing needs if your book is already written, however it can be done.

Ideally, I love to work with writers in the beginning stages to build each section or chapter with a marketing strategy in mind. This mindset will save you lots of time and give a clear direction on the different ways to use and sell your material. A little planning goes a long way here. It also will simplify the writing journey and make it specific to those who vitally need your information and future products.

A great example of how to include a particular marketing idea within your book is to intentionally write a chapter that can later be positioned as an opt-in free download on your website. In addition to including your url in your book, you can use this tool to drive more traffic to your site and naturally build your database. A particular chapter or several different chapters can also be sold as individual eBooks for a fragment of the cost of your entire book.

You can also apply this idea by simply using a list of questions, benefits, solutions or important sets of tools you may offer in your book and provide a free consultation for another service. It makes me crazy when I see an author place their book on Amazon for a certain price and then offer the entire book as an eBook for pennies! I am surprised as to how many people will offer their work for just a few dollars. There are many ways to give something away for free without giving away the store!

I also find the reason that so many writers and authors don't like to focus on their market is because they want to stay in the creative flow of writing and producing other products. I place no judgment on anyone here but wish to make a few distinctions as simple observations. My experience has shown me that a good majority of writers and authors are not business-minded individuals and will often down play the value they bring to the table.

In fact, a small number of them would sooner give away their books for free than to strategize a marketing solution that would make them money. In addition, a few will go as far as to say that people can't afford to buy their twenty dollar book, not knowing they are projecting this limiting thought onto their market.

I honestly believe that one can sell their market short by downplaying the value of their work. Generally speaking, people expect to pay for what they need or mostly want so why should your book or potential products and services be any different?

Needless to say, this is why I like to uncover as much information as possible in our initial consultation. As a Book Marketing Acceleration Coach and Mentor, I love to witness what happens when people break free of some of these limiting thoughts. I also acknowledge that they have to have the willingness to be successful authors and authorpreneurs. There is no reason for anyone to put their time and effort into a book that can't be sold, unless it is the very rare exception of a legacy generational-type book that is personal and meant only for members of a family.

Step into The Mindset of the *Already* Successful Authorpreneur

Has it ever occurred to you that you can grow your book concept or idea into a multimillion or multibillion dollar business? Chances are if you've picked up this book, you are already ahead of the game! I congratulate you because it is not the norm for people to approach writing a book with the idea of creating a business around it, much less having the mindset of potentially making millions.

The idea of being a published author sometimes takes over the writer, through no fault of their own. I know the feeling well and have lived the experience of the exuberance that comes with a finished product, especially after three rewrites and waiting five years! However, I must say that there is so much more than racing to get onto Amazon and into the bookstores! This is primarily why I like to have in-depth conversations with writers and authors *before* they write their books.

I know it may sound silly to say this, but it's so important to get curious as to how to expand or grow your book concept so it will make you money—lots of it! Most overnight success stories are based on years of preparation. Now, I'm here to tell you that it need not take several years due to the fact that many writers have paved the way for you. Having access to our wonderful worldwide web and its capabilities allows us to take quantum leaps with some of the most successful marketing strategies and models.

One of the things that I like to focus on with my clients is to go where their greatest excitement takes them. This makes the actual book writing experience a breeze as the book tends to write itself through the passion of the individual. What usually excites writers is the experience of growing their confidence and seeing the bigger picture. It's amazing to witness the magic that occurs for them as they follow that excitement.

They start to experience their project take on a life of its own. People start coming out of nowhere to suddenly support their work. It is within the excitement that they attract more of it as in the law of attraction. Opportunities find you when you are naturally vibrating at higher frequencies. It is simply one of the universal laws at work!

Regardless of what your book is or going to be about, taking on the mindset of one who has already achieved success will catapult you in record time. Remember, the meaning you give success and how you create it in your mind is completely yours; it shouldn't be compared to the mindset of anyone else.

Do you remember the very first time you achieved something really significant? If so, you probably had to step out of yourself and into being a whole new you. You may have also pictured or visualized another professional doing that very same thing you had to do and just for a moment imagined what it would be like to be them.

Let me explain: as part of one of the "101 Ways to Honor Yourself as a Woman" listed in my first book, *In Honor of Women*, I decided I would personally take voice lessons since I was your typical shower singer and horrified about singing anywhere in public.

I decided I would take a class just as soon as I could find a good one. Well, to my surprise, I soon discovered the truth within the old saying, "The teacher appears when the student is ready." To my greatest astonishment, one of the most amazing voice teachers appeared effortlessly in my life. She actually came to teach the yoga masters at my yoga class as a group and opened up the class to the members of the center.

Now, I must preface this by telling you I was completely clueless when it came to my voice or anything about it. I had tried a couple of different teachers in Los Angeles but didn't really feel a connection with them at the time. However, Betty Forte had a particular brilliance and a profound sense of grace about her that blessed each and every student in her class.

I can't tell you how excited I was about attending my first class. I had attempted being part of a choir for a short time but always felt extremely self-conscious, which usually led me to getting sore throats due to voice straining. Well, Betty suggested we take the first week and visit a sheet music store to select one of our favorite songs. I had heard a beautiful Italian aria, "O Mio Babbino Caro" composed by Puccini on a commercial and decided I'd bring that one to class the next week.

To show you just how clueless I was, I thought she wanted to get a sense of what kind of music we liked or teach us more about the music itself. After working with the scales, she took a few minutes to visit with each of the seven students. I handed her my song when she got to me.

As she looked at my music and CD that accompanied it, she said, "Great! Now, Darlin, I want you to practice this song because you're going to sing it in four weeks!" I must have looked at her as if she was from another planet because her words didn't quite register with my brain. This was an operatic piece. I couldn't even sing in a choir and she expected me to sing an aria?! I attempted to convince her that this was a *really* bad idea, but that didn't work very well. Betty had a way of asking that made it hard to say, "No" to her.

So, there I was practicing my song in my car, my living room and of course, the shower. The only thing about it that was familiar was the Italian language while everything else was beyond foreign to me. Needless to say, just the thought of singing opera in front of everyone by the fourth class was enough to send me into shakes of sheer terror! But with every class leading toward the moment of truth, Betty somehow gave me a little more confidence and guts. I found her method of teaching very interesting as she helped me feel empowered instead of horribly petrified!

What happened next still sends chills up my spine. I remember shaking like a leaf during a bad storm with sweat rising out of the pores on my forehead. I literally shook as my voice seemed to come from the depths of Mother Earth, herself. It was one of the most unbelievable experiences of my life. Though the song only lasted a little over two minutes, it felt like it went on for an eternity as I stood there in front of everyone!

Now, what I didn't know was that there had been lying within me a completely dormant voice that no one had *ever* heard—not even me! Honestly, there is no explanation for gifts that truly come from the heavens, and this gift completely shocked me as well as those who heard me. With every class my skills and voice grew stronger. I quickly learned that the reason I didn't think I could ever sing was because I had too much vibrato in my voice, which in turn is perfect for opera!

I soon graduated to private lessons with Betty as she classically trained me to confidently reach those high notes that she referred to as high frequency notes. Her way of teaching made me love to vocally soar to some of the highest summits and just hang there for a while!

To my most humble amazement, I was performing professionally within two years in California and later also performed in Italy. I share this part of my life with you because sometimes there are extraordinary gifts just waiting to be discovered when we continue to walk through those doors of excitement. I also share it because I learned from Betty that I needed to step into a new expanded sense of myself in order to perform for an audience. I had been comfortable with public speaking since I was nineteen but this…this was a whole new world for me.

She prepared me by having myself imagine being on stage and literally stepping into the shoes of a world renowned opera singer. Usually it was one of my favorite singers: Maria Callas or Renée Fleming. She would ask me to feel their confidence within me and to *really* feel it as if I were them. She used to laugh as she often said I was unconsciously competent. I often wondered if she knew the power of her teaching. Betty taught me that the secret to success is to literally step into it, feel it and be it with every cell of my body.

I practiced that visualization and exercise countless times, especially right before a performance until I could own it as an integral part of myself. I now had a whole new mindset separate from that person who once was afraid to have anyone hear her. I was now a *completely* different person. Although both Betty Forte and my dear Italian maestro, Vittorio Bari, have graced the Heavens above, they will forever be my beloved Angels. They are always and will forever be present in my heart, especially when I sing!

So, I ask you, who do you need to be to get to the next level in your life? What do you need to feel to be that person? What are your dreams?

You may be surprised to find that what you need already lives within you. It is said that if you have at least ten thousand hours of study and experience in any one particular subject matter, then in fact you are considered a master on that topic and especially in your profession. Just thought to share that with you because it always surprises me to find the vast amount of knowledge lying within a person that is so often overlooked! It's funny how the person who often says, "Do I have enough or know enough information to fill a book of a couple hundred pages?" will usually exceed that page count to their own amazement!

This is certainly my own opinion, but as soon as a person gets the idea to write a book, that book already exists! In fact, I believe most people have many books within them. It doesn't matter what your background is or what degrees you have or don't have, your knowledge is certainly worth sharing—especially if it can provide something of value to someone else.

If you already have a business and want to write a book on the topic of your business, this will most certainly increase your revenue stream—not to mention give you lots of credibility. So for example, if you are an expert in your field and have already had at least a decade of experience, you can easily position yourself as an authority.

Chances are you may have developed systems or solution-based ways of doing things that can help a fellow expert in your field. A simple yet powerful idea is to write your *million dollar seed* in a way that offers solutions as a leading expert to other professionals in your industry. With the concepts in your book, you can develop countless online training programs, in-person or online teleseminars, and host blog radio talk shows—just to name a few!

To be successful in the world of books, it is important to do what many others have already done. There's no sense in reinventing the wheel! For example, well-known authors will train other executive coaches to teach their programs and in turn earn a percentage of every ongoing training program. This beautifully allows the author the freedom to work less while continuing to create more products that can enhance those programs. Think of how many coaches and trainers are out there that would love to train with you and help you share your message and concepts.

Think of the potential for the back-of-the-room sales with several people giving your workshops and selling your products! Charging the coaches for your training will certainly add to your cash flow, and you can dictate how many coaches you want to train in a variety of locations based on your desired income. Ideally, it is best to select coaches who already have a following so those workshops can be offered online as teleseminars as well as potentially grow into a live event! In addition, each teleseminar can be recorded and sold to each audience member!

The key here is to start thinking out of the box in order to use your knowledge in ways that can make life easier for others and help you create wealth. The things that come the easiest to us are the very things we can charge the most for because those are the very things that are challenging or difficult for others. It's never about ego, but it is about knowing the value we bring to the table and what that looks like for others.

I know several bestselling authors who started out giving workshops *without* a book, which gave them a great opportunity to learn more about their market. Those workshops and events helped them make a living while working another job. The more workshops they gave, the easier it became to create and offer new products and books. The back-of-the-room sales became a very integral aspect of their business because their audiences expected to purchase products every time they attended their events.

Are you ready to provide your market with what they need? The more you know about your audience, the easier it is to create those products for them and forecast others as you go based on your personally tailored timeline. You can train yourself to listen for the questions coming from your audiences that will address and benefit the most number of people. Those questions are where you look for products that speak to their problems and challenges for personal and/or business growth.

At times it is both personal and business related, but the key is to stay open and aware of the possibilities and opportunities that will present themselves. Get REALLY curious as to what you can do next so you can keep yourself sharp and in the momentum of success. Feel your power and know that if others can do it, so can you!

One of the important questions I love to ask a potential client is, "How much money would you like to make as part of your vision with this book, product or service your first year?" I find many are pleasantly surprised by this question because they really haven't given it much thought. How can we build a business with your book or build an empire if we don't have an idea of what you want to earn? Nothing pleases me more than to create strategies that can support a specific financial decision and desired outcome. It is so much fun to align one's skill-set with a plan of products, services and action items.

It is noteworthy to mention that the topic of your desired income will be touched on throughout *The Million Dollar Seed*. It is truly a major component and inspiration to contributing your information not only as a book, but as a powerful business. The idea of your desired income is naturally fed with the thought of building your business with an authorpreneur mindset. As mentioned before, placing value on what you offer and knowing who you are offering it to is what many authors struggle with, which can be very detrimental to their bottom line!

It is very common for writers to answer my question, "Who are you writing this book for?" with "Everyone!" This answer tells me that this individual has not taken the time to really identify their market, which will without a doubt lower their chances for success. Not knowing *exactly* whom you are writing for makes it hard to know your market's needs, wants and desires.

Having an idea of whom your market is targeting simply isn't enough! Remember, your audience is looking to you to be an authority in your field. As an author, you *must* position yourself as that authority and come from a strong place of reference, knowledge and recommendation for them. Your audience is waiting for you to offer your knowledge in a way that makes sense to them. But none of that can happen unless you know exactly who you are writing for! Go ahead—take the authorpreneur's hat and try it on for size!

I often tell the story of the jeweler who had a ton of right hand diamond rings in stock that he really wanted to sell in order to make room for other merchandise. At the time, I was working with business owners throughout the country to help them with their online marketing needs; I helped them increase their sales by showing them how to sell more of their showcased items.

When I asked him to whom he was selling the rings, he replied, "Everyone!" Once I realized he had all of these beautiful rings to sell, I suggested he ask his web designer to place all of the images of the right handed rings in stock on one page, add "right handed diamond rings" to his SEO tag words for his site and create a link for that phrase. This link would take people directly to that page instead of his home page. Though he initially resisted, he called within a few weeks to tell me that his sales skyrocketed!

Identifying and being as specific as possible with whom your market is targeting gives you one hundred percent of their attention as to the nominal attention you get when you market to everyone. It seems like such a simple thing, but so many miss the success that is waiting to be had! Think of how you look for what you need at any given moment. Do you go online and do a Google search, and if so, how specific are you with your search words or phrases? Chances are you are very specific and know exactly what you are looking for! This is an example of how people find what they are looking for. The value in knowing what your market needs is what gives you a huge advantage.

Many writers come to me at different stages of writing or even publication. Without a doubt, almost ten times out of ten, the most frequent commonality that is a miss is the marketing component. Hence the reason I personally felt the need and great desire to contribute this body of work.

Here are Ten of the Most Common Marketing Mistakes Made by Writers and Authors Who Write Self-Help and Industry Specific Solution-Based Books:

1. Write without knowing who they are writing for: their audience's issues, needs and desires

2. Write without a marketing strategy in place and miss the opportunity to introduce their website, products, programs, and services within contents

3. Download their knowledge instead of giving their audience an experience

4. Base their writing on their own needs instead of the needs of their readers, in addition to not writing with a business mindset

5. Don't include enough heartfelt stories that specifically relate to their audience

6. Expect the reader to know more than they know

7. Miss the opportunity to create credibility with profound success stories

8. Choose a title that is not specific to the content, and instead place more emphasis on the subtitle causing them to repeatedly have to explain what the book is about!

9. Often overlook the main component of providing and identifying solutions in a simple three-step or odd numbered step format for their audience

10. Write their introduction first instead of last

These mistakes are made often because most writers aren't aware of what they don't know when they get the bug to write a book. However, don't kick yourself if you didn't know this in the event that you have already written or published a book. Honestly, there were a lot of things I didn't know when I was writing *In Honor of Women.* Looking back, I may have entitled it something different potentially based on a positive call to action, but I will get into titles later.

I changed my table of contents over and over because I didn't have a marketing strategy in place, which forced me to have to rewrite my introduction at least a dozen times. As much as I loved adding or changing a chapter to make it better, I absolutely hated to have to rewrite my introduction again! On the other hand, it was easy to give my audience an experience with some of the stories based on my study and findings. Thank goodness I got that one right!

For me, reading a good book is a lot like watching a good movie. Whenever I think of one of my favorite books, I think of all of the different emotions and experiences I had while reading it. I usually walk away feeling really great inside, and sometimes—when it's really good—the feeling is with me every time I think of it. As writers, we need to remember our writing is all about pleasing our readers and our audiences. Make your takeaways memorable for them like never before! Give them everything; even if it has to be done in parts—make *every* part rich and abundant for them. In short, we write for them *first* and then ourselves.

Think about your market for a moment as you read the following. Why do we as authors write books?

We write books to serve, to inspire, to fill the gap where it is needed, to support where there isn't enough, to show we care, to feel their triumphs as well as to identify with their pain, to provide them with cutting edge solutions, offer business trade secrets, to make their lives easier than our lives, to give them the courage to live their dreams, to teach what is working now, to offer something to a particular niche that may be overlooked, to bring out the best in them, and so much more!

Whatever reason caused your heart to light up while reading is where you may find the stirrings or beginnings for the benefits and solutions to provide your market. It's all about resonating with your audience and coming from your heart, which leads me back to the importance of sharing your stories within your *million dollar seed!*

There are two ways most people like to write: one is to write factually with very little emotion (what I call *downloading*) and the other is to write from an experience that allows the reader the benefit of all of the feelings behind that experience. We want to take them on a journey—hopefully one that lingers for some time to come!

Dave Bartholomew, author of *The Diamond Principle*: *The CEO's Common-Sense, Time-Tested 21st Century Guide to Making Can't-Miss Decisions and Getting Things Done,* came to me a couple of years ago with zip files of information he wanted to use in his book. Once I was able to understand exactly who his audience was, his skillset, his *why* and vision, I soon realized his book needed to take on an entirely different form than that of which he was thinking! I gathered very quickly that the information in those files was not practical for the book he wanted to write, nor was it easy for the average CEO to grasp!

Given the technical aspects of his knowledge, his writing needed to be fun, light and packed with a common sense approach for CEOs of medium to large companies. We provided his readers with his significant success stories which are still very impressive to me. In addition, these stories reinforced the value within his work and contributed a new facet of confidence for him.

We also made it easy for his target market, being CEOs, to quickly understand the benefits of retaining him as a consultant; this was his ultimate desired outcome and one of the main reasons for writing his book.

I share this story because it is a great example of how easy it is to use text (factual) information in either book or speaking form. It is a sure thing that anytime someone downloads or uses text information, we tend to tune them out. Have you ever listened to someone speak that didn't offer any stories or just told you what to do as part of their expertise? Well, the fact is that some writers like to do the same thing and forget to share their experiences for fear that they will bore their readers.

Actually it is quite the opposite! Because we live in a world that constantly feeds us information, we as authors and speakers have a bigger responsibility to share our rich content in a fun, comprehensive, and experiential way. *News Flash*: our readers and audiences want to connect with us. They want to know our stories and relate to us through them. In fact, they respect those who have walked the walk before them.

At the beginning, I sometimes need to remind my writers to offer anecdotes because most of us remember stories that relate to what we are learning! Had Dave included most of what was in those files, chances are very few people—if any—would identify with the material. Restructuring the information to make it more appealing and experiential made all the difference in the world for him and his market audience!

Authors will often come to me with their published works on Amazon needing to create a plan on how to sell their books. In order to serve them properly, I immediately take them back to their *why* behind their concept, then I explore their skillset and vision before identifying a marketing strategy for their book. At the end of the day, it's all about positive exposure through a variety of avenues and streams to increase awareness for your market that is also known as your tribe.

I strongly recommend knowing everything you can about the individuals that will benefit from your work. If your *million dollar seed* is industry specific or self-development based, then you will need to provide some solutions that speak to their issues, problems and concerns.

Here Are Fifteen Questions to Help You Identify How You Can Best Support The People You Wish to Serve Before Writing Your *Million Dollar Seed.*

1. What are some of the major problems my reader and market is facing right now?
2. How old are they?
3. What do they believe?
4. Is there something I can develop as a tool for them?

5. Is my book idea one that works for men and women, or would it be better for one gender?
6. Can this book idea also work for teenagers and/or children and/or boomers?
7. What online solutions can I create for them?
8. Is there a package, product or service that I can sell the most of to a specific audience?
9. If they could have one product that would make their life easier, what would it be?
10. Are they stuck in a particular mindset where I can help them break free?
11. Will my information help them get clear on what is possible based on my experience?
12. What would I have paid for someone to have offered me this information when I needed it the most?
13. How can I help them improve their lives?
14. What clear and concise solutions can I offer them?
15. How can I save them time, money, frustration, disappointment, etc. with what I have to offer?

These questions are some of the most important questions you could ever ask yourself as a writer and author who is truly interested in helping those who really need you and your products. Although every one of them is significant, the one that teaches us the most about our own sense of self-worth and how to give our products and services a price or fee is question twelve. The insight gained by most with this question is indescribable! The answer to this question is often the first time that an individual really gets the value they bring to the table for the people in their marketplace.

Test Your Market

If you don't have a business that you are basing your book on, this is all the more of a reason to find several ways to test your market. So, what do I mean by testing your market? It's a really good idea to start a focus group or select a handful of people that can support you with your writing or your *why.* Now when you select these individuals, make sure they aren't related to you or your best friends. You want professionals or people who know more than you regarding your market.

For example, if you are writing a children's book with an emotional development lesson and you don't have any children yourself, you wouldn't ask your mother to be part of this focus group. With all due respect to Mom, you would want to consider bringing in teachers, child psychologists, caretakers, doctors, etc. for the appropriate age group that you are selling to since these are the professionals who work directly with the parents that could potentially purchase your book.

I would also seek out a C-Level manager of a corporation to be part of this group that once again relates to your message or book. Have that CEO or an educational director of a children's corporation or organization give you feedback on the benefits of your book or book series. There is a specific reason why you want to be very mindful while choosing these individuals.

The key is to approach these individuals with the possibility of selling your *million dollar seed* by the bulk to them or at least a few of them. More to come on bulk sales in a bit, however; planting these ideas here will help you with your approach to a broader spectrum of marketing ideas.

Having a focus group helps you work out all of the cobwebs that may exist within the material. I usually suggest either twenty minute to half hour Skype calls with everyone on board for a quick meeting on some specific feedback that you need in order to ensure you are on the right track with your market. Based on your own level of confidence in your material and product, you will determine your expectations and timeline with these individuals.

You may choose to have three meetings with them beginning with a quick questionnaire or conversation prior to starting your project. Make sure that you have everyone sign a non-disclosure agreement as your idea and concepts need to remain confidential within this group so that your work can be acknowledged as *your* intellectual property. We will touch on the legal aspects later.

Typically, it is best to ask them how they prefer to be part of your group as some prefer only email while others prefer Skype or conference calls. Once you have that information, then you can decide the best way to approach each individual.

Once you have your focus group in place, you can also ask specific questions about your market. In the case of the children's book writer, you would want to know as much as you could about the parents as they are primarily the main market. You would want to know age, income, interests, what is and isn't working regarding your particular concept, etc.

In addition to all of that, you want to make it available for your focus group to help steer your product so that they may see it as something beneficial for their clients, patients, customer, etc. Once again, it is all about being open to their feedback as they are experts in the field and will have a pulse on what is currently needed from your market.

When you feel your book is ready, then you can offer a few copies to each individual on your focus team to pass along to their clients, patients and customers for feedback. They will then know who to give it to for their input. You'll want to keep each person accountable to a desired time frame, such as a couple of weeks. If too much time passes, you may lose your momentum with them. It needs to be established that the input or feedback from the parents and children (as part of this example) is a contribution to you as the author. I have found that most people are very receptive to offering their feedback, especially when it comes to helping an author.

Using the same example of the children's book, testing the market can also allow you to take it to a school and build your results. You may find that your book can grow into a learning program for a particular grade school level.

One of my dearest clients, Kimberlee Schultz who authored *The StarPals™ Series* of books for children ages 3-7, beautifully exemplifies how one simple concept can easily grow into several products. Each of her books focuses on inspiring and empowering children to embrace a specific virtue with a particular virtue character. Kimberlee took the series to a school to test it with children in a classroom. Both the children and teachers absolutely adored these books and characters! I loved getting the call from her as she shared her experience with the children.

I remember the first testimonial she received from a friend of hers who has twins. The twins were three or four years old at the time, and their mother had read *Patty Patience*, the first of *The StarPals™ Book Series*, to them. While getting out of her van, she noticed the boys were unusually quiet, and when she opened the slider door she found them sitting patiently with their hands on their laps. Clearly this was highly unusual as they were seldom this quiet. When she asked what was going on, they replied, "We're playing the *Patty Patience* game, Mommy!" Like so many other parents, Kimberlee's friend couldn't wait to get the rest of the series.

From that experience and many others, Kimberlee developed the Social Emotional Empowerment Development (SEED) Platform for children. The site coordinators for LA's BEST After School Program serve approximately 186 inner city schools for the LA Unified School District. Kimberlee, with The StarPals™ SEED Platform, has collaborated with LA's BEST to create a BEST Practices Model featuring The StarPals™ Series to support a variety of learning styles; these styles can be implemented at any private, public or home school nationwide. There's a lot more to share about this particular author and series as we dive deeper into building your business with products and programs.

When we look at testing a product in your market, we're actually just trying it out to see what kind of a response you get from your audience. A good example is to select a small number of people out of your database and do a mini launch to see what works instead of sending it to your entire database. It's just a way to get a response. If it is a product that you can offer a certain number of people, you may want to have a questionnaire or something in place for them to fill out. Testing your market gives you a chance to tweak what may need a little more polishing or clarification before offering it to the masses.

Fall In Love *with* Your Market

When you take the time to study whom you're writing for, it's easy to fall in love with them. Seeing how happy and grateful the parents and caretakers are with Kimberlee's books makes both of our hearts soar with happiness. She really has done an incredible job in creating a strong empowerment series and platform for children. Kimberlee makes it fun for children to build and strengthen their social emotional skills while positively impacting their home, school and community around them.

Seeing my clients experience success and live their dream is why I do what I do! There is such a wonderful rippling effect when we adore our clients and do everything we can to genuinely serve them. In doing so, they shine brilliantly in their own magnificence that overflows onto the people they serve in their markets.

Though I am approached by many writers and authors who have an idea for a book or have already written one, I don't say yes to everyone. I only choose to work with those who want to write books that are going to have a positive impact on their designated market(s).

I have an affinity for those who are authentic, loving in nature, and very committed to the needs of their target market. For me, it's all about the writers and authors who are passionate about sharing their message. It's about those who want to learn more about their audience and are willing to help them. They may not start out knowing who they are specifically serving, but I know their heart is in the right place. I can usually tell within the first fifteen minutes of our conversation as to whether we are a good match.

Do you, like many authors, consider it a privilege to work with your tribe or market? If you do, you will find your work to be very gratifying, and at times will feel like it's not work at all. So often it is easy to overlook the simplest of things like the value that both our clients and markets bring us, sometimes on a daily basis.

Nothing pleases me more than to receive an email from one of my clients that highlights an accolade for their work. This particular client happened to be on vacation in South Africa when he emailed me his great news. I could feel his excitement as the words jumped off my computer screen. It was so incredible!

Steve Schloss, author of *The Man's Secret™ to A Happy and Sexy Marriage in Less Than Ten Minutes a Day*, had been in the market testing stages with his book. He sent one of his many solutions, "101 Ways To A Sexy Marriage", to his focus group.

As it turned out, one of the individuals emailed "The 101 Ways" to his cousin who had a remarkable breakthrough! The gentleman went on to say that Steve has a goldmine as his book will help not only men who have been married for many years, but also help the young married men who have hit a wall! This speaks volumes to the benefits of testing your market, and how it assists with your connection to your readers. As I refer to falling in love with the people in your market, I am speaking directly to building your relationship with them.

It is extraordinary to get to a place where our readers experience a real sense of accomplishment when the accolades build upon themselves in the form of sales. It is also powerful to help them break free of whatever is in their way. When you come from a place of experience regarding what most of your audience fears, it can be helpful to remember your own.

I can easily recall feeling so nervous about sharing my writing for the first time and all of the negative thoughts that ran through my head—or the first time I spoke in front of an audience. I thought I was going to get sick as I felt my heart in my throat! Like many, my own experiences have helped me fully understand what others are going through and how to guide them past their fears, doubts and worries.

So, when I say to fall in love with your market, I mean to fall in love with helping the individuals within your audiences get to *their* next! See for them what they can't see for themselves. They will bless you in return with an amazing sense of loyalty, and deep appreciation for all that you do for them.

Find Your Market and Audience

Knowing your audience doesn't mean you'll always know where to find them. However, if you have a sense as to their interests, you will find they hang out where they can learn the most or be part of what is important to them. For example, you may find them at trade shows, conventions for certain industry specific corporations or companies, workshops, industry specific bloggers, online events, radio blog talk shows that speak to a variety of topics, motivational speakers' events, live events, for profit and non-profit organizations, etc.

The key is to go where they go! So often, we

surround ourselves with networks regarding our message; we also surround ourselves with groups that are not truly related to our markets and real target audiences. Going this route makes it really tough and not nearly as productive as being where they are! There is an abundance of events for most industries and markets, many of which are annually held in various parts of the country and world.

The most important way to the top of any bestseller list is to develop and build relationships with multiple people who have or belong to large networks; they may naturally be interested in the countless branches that stem from your topic or topics. We'll get into more of this as we get further along in these chapters.

Finding your audience will also help you align with like-minded people for joint venturing and collaborative efforts. Look for them everywhere you can imagine finding them. Finding an online topic tied to your interests that committed bloggers are interacting with is also a great example of where to look!

"How becomes obsolete when you make the decision to get what you want!"

– Stella Togo

CHAPTER 3

GET PAID WHILE YOU WRITE YOUR MILLION DOLLAR SEED

Can you imagine getting paid as an expert in your field while you write your book? Well, the truth is many bestselling authors have started out that way, even while taking a basic side job just to pay the bills. There are countless ways of getting paid while you write that can be tied to the book you are currently working on!

Once again, it is important to look where your heart lights up, especially around your skill-set and the platform you wish to create for yourself. If you love to teach, what would you love to bring forward as a class, workshop, teleseminar, etc.? You could even test it out with a few people for a fraction of the price you would charge for the full event. What part of your book could you possibly sell as an eBook? You could choose to have your event online, allowing you to work from anywhere without cost.

Another possibility is to prerecord your work and offer it a number of times to a variety of groups.

Community colleges will pay you to teach a class, which is a great way to get your material together and get accustomed to presenting it. I really enjoyed teaching book writing to both college students and children in elementary schools. I highly recommend offering a class because it gives you a solid experience, especially if you are interested in positioning yourself as a speaker and trainer. I absolutely loved both levels and found it very rewarding on many fronts.

I had the privilege of having a blind man as one of my students who helped me stretch in ways beyond my imagination. He taught me the real significance of seeing from the heart. Today, I am able to bring that to my coaching and show writers how to put feeling behind their words in order to provide color for their stories and messages.

The children utterly astonished me with their willingness to learn how to write a series of books and how to publish them. I often wonder who learned more in the classes I taught: my students or me! Teaching was by far one of the greatest experiences, and I feel blessed to have done it.

If you are currently writing a book, you can list a variety of topics that relate to your work and start blogging for your market. As you blog on these topics, it may be easier to pull some takeaways that can be brought to a classroom, workshop or online course. Look for a way to consolidate your information into a solution-based format with an odd number. For example, you can identify some of the takeaways and lead with steps, tools, ways, secrets, etc. You may naturally develop this information into a home study program that you can also sell as an additional product.

If you can imagine yourself as a coach or consultant for a specific niche, why not try it out on a part-time basis? Create three simple packages that speak to three specific needs you can fulfill for your clients. As you work the packages, you will find it easier to fine tune them based on the results you experience with your clients. Assisting writers to create and develop their coaching packages is so enjoyable because it allows looking for creative ways to offer solutions to their potential clients.

One particular type of package that seems to work well for both coaches and their clients are the private half day and full day VIP packages that allow the client to have the coach completely to themselves for four to six hours. These packages are designed and custom tailored to meet the specific needs of the client in a very condensed format. The beauty of coaching is that it can be done on Skype or online as well as the phone. All of my coaching is done either on the phone or on Skype based on the location of my clients.

I love coaching this way because it allows me to hear so much more than when I have the person in front of me as there is little risk for distraction. It also allows me to do my calls back to back on the days I coach my clients.

Position Yourself as a Leading Expert

Keep in mind there is no room for shyness when it comes to being a leading expert in your field. It is expected of you to stand tall with what you believe in when teaching your audience regardless of the platform you choose for yourself. People have a keen sense for identifying an individual who comes from integrity and authenticity verses one who is a little murky in their own conviction.

People look to us for honest guidance as thought leaders, experts, authors and speakers. If we expect to be effective with our designated markets, we must come from tremendous confidence and strength. It is always more about them than it is about us.

When writing or developing your books and products, don't be shy about making strong suggestions based on your convictions and beliefs. Now, there is a distinction between making a suggestion and speaking down to your readers. Keep in mind, as leading authorities it is our job to offer our suggestions while giving them an opportunity to embrace and relate to our knowledge. The way I have found to avoid coming off as egotistical is to stay focused on their needs and do the best to come from the heart. I often suggest to writers that the best approach is to offer the information in such a way that makes one ponder and helps promote thinking.

We may start with our knowledge first to build our products and services for them. However, we also need to look at our appearance and how we present ourselves to our audience. I see it often where someone has an incredible knowledge base but their appearance is terribly distracting, so it makes it hard for the listener to stay focused on the delivery. There is something to be said about aligning your professional clothing style or image with your inner confidence. Walking onto a stage dressed in one of my most professional suits usually enhances my confidence level. Though many of you may already know this, it is worth mentioning as it is so important to be polished on every front.

Shortly after my second edition of *In Honor of Women* was released by Ballantine Books in 1998, I had an opportunity to speak by phone with Oprah's producers for several weeks. At the time, Oprah had a segment on her show called "Remembering The Spirit" in which they were looking to bring me on for the following fall season. This segment was featured at the end of the show and highlighted ordinary people who had been involved in extraordinary situations. Her producer at the time was exploring the possibility of me sharing my story and personal study with other breast cancer survivors.

Their focus was for me to share with the audience how I overcame adversity so as to inspire viewers to do the same in their own lives. Well, I can't begin to tell you how exciting and terrifying those weeks were for me! I had to be up before dawn (because I live in the West Coast) and ready to answer a variety of questions by 5 am PDT, since the meetings were held in central time.

Now, I couldn't speak with Oprah's producers in my nighty so I would throw on a blazer over my nighty, along with a pair of high heeled pumps, and quickly put on some lipstick. Then I would run downstairs, grab my coffee and mentally prepare for my conversation.

The funny thing was, my daughter who was about six at the time came downstairs after one of my meetings. She looked at me strangely while rubbing her eyes and said, "Mommy, you're not going to work like *that* are you?" I still remember her sweet little face and perplexed look as she knew something was definitely off! I scooped her up and said, "No Honey, I just had a phone call." As fate would have it, they ended up changing the show that fall and dropped that segment. Well, there's always next time! Regardless, it was an experience I will never forget! There was something about putting on that jacket and shoes that made me feel ready and confident! What is in your wardrobe that would make you feel ready to speak with Oprah's producers at 5 am?

If you were to look at your skills and loves, how would you like to position yourself? When you think of yourself speaking with people, what is the image that comes to mind? Who do you see yourself speaking with? What do you feel as you let your mind hang there for a minute? If you could choose to speak with anyone, who would that person be? Would you speak with them in person, and where are you? If I could make a difference in the world, how would I do it? Now the key question to ask yourself is, "Who do I need to be to be that person?"

I am living proof that when we combine imagination with desire and the discipline to take action, we can do most anything! I believe it is in our imagination that we find the magic in our lives, and having the courage to live out that magic takes discipline. Yes, it takes daily discipline to focus on what we want as I am constantly training myself. We come into this world with open eyes and immense curiosity to learn with joy. What took me a while to understand is that it is in the joy of learning and staying really curious that makes it easy to focus on our heart's desire.

Since we have choice and free will, we can choose at any given moment to look for the gifts in the darkest hour or a little glimmer of light in a situation where there seemingly is none. Looking for those gifts naturally drives us into curiosity, which organically opens us up to what is possible in life.

Daydreaming is simply another word for visualization, allowing us to step into our happiness and greatest joy. I find it interesting that when we take time to go there, all worries, fears and doubts fall away because they simply can't co-exist in the world of imagination—and it indeed truly is a world in its own right. If you don't believe me, try watching one of Walt Disney's classics while being worried about something. A couple of my favorite films I loved to watch with my son were *Jungle Book* and *Pinocchio*. It still warms my heart as I remember his contagious baby belly laughs!

My point is I believe the greater part of excelling at most anything is to be open to our greatest imagination. We can easily build on a skillset or take a public speaking class, or learn many new skills. However, learning from our imagination and giving ourselves the permission to go after what we see with our mind's eye makes it easier to bring it into reality.

A book gives a business owner, a leading expert, or an inspired author opportunities to walk through many different doors. The idea that you took the time to write for someone else and care enough about people to develop your knowledge for them really gives you credibility in every sense of the word. Most people look up to authors for that very reason. There is a true sense of appreciation for published authors because the general population knows it takes a lot for most people to write their books.

As an expert author, one of the many opportunities that are available to you is to become a blog talk radio show host. For example, if you like working from your home office and don't want to necessarily be in front of an audience, this is a wonderful way to reach your audience.

This is why it is good to know your strengths and what feels right to you. What works for one person may not work as well for someone else. The sky is the limit if you have the willingness to explore the possibilities as potential opportunities. Having a blog talk radio show can give you a chance to test some of the information you are looking to include in your book. The key is to create and develop a following that you can count on time after time. Having your own show as an author will also give you a leg up on finding other local and non-local authors to collaborate with on a variety of topics that relate to one another.

Another option is to conduct interviews while videotaping people who can contribute to your topic. Placing the videos on your website will do two things for you and the person you interview: It will speak volumes as people will see you as an authority in your field and the interviewee will have an opportunity to plug their business—especially if they have a book, product or upcoming event. You can charge your interviewees since you will be plugging their business, and you can also sell the interviews as a separate product—particularly if they have celebrity-status.

With over seventy hours of radio interviews as part of my initial book launch, I found my interviews got easier and easier over time. I learned to share some of the questions I knew I could easily answer in a timely fashion. In fact, it was fun when I could share my list of questions prior to the interview because it took guessing out of what would transpire in those few minutes. On the other hand, it was also fun to get a livewire-personality type with lots of energy and passion for my air time.

Needless to say, the sky is the limit as to how many channels are available to expert authors these days. The idea is to find those channels that best fit your personality. At the end of the day, it's all about the joy you find in doing what you're doing regardless of how you're doing it. That said, I do think it is important to try new things and stretch whenever possible because what may be around the corner is the very thing that will change your life and profoundly impact your audience in an extraordinary way!

Just yesterday I spoke with a woman who has happily completed her book. Within our brief consultation, we went from her potentially making five hundred dollars a month as part of her vision to the possibility of setting herself up as a trainer and earning ten thousand dollars a month.

To my amazement, she had traveled the world and had been a leading expert as part of her missionary work for more than four decades. Her background easily positions her for the potential of not only being an expert author and trainer, but also gaining greater financial successes that will in turn help her grow her philanthropic endeavors at a much faster pace. It is so exciting to look at the countless opportunities that are available for writers, authors, trainers and speakers!

"When we start with the end goal in mind, the next step is easy!"

– Stella Togo

CHAPTER 4

PLANT YOUR MILLION DOLLAR SEED

Ever wonder why anyone would ever consider writing a book without planning for their desired outcome or having an idea for their desired income? Imagine taking a job where you had no indication of how much money you would earn, who you were working for or how long it would take you to complete that job?

Many writers and authors will spend years writing and rewriting their books without knowing or planning their marketing strategies for their potential financial success. In fact, most people are initially so overwhelmed by just the idea of where to begin that going much further than that seems literally impossible!

Chances are you may feel like you can't even imagine taking the time for all that! It is my opinion; however, that the old adage of how knowledge is everything rings true based on the countless writers and published authors I've spoken with throughout the years. Knowing how to approach book writing from a financially rewarding mindset can make your efforts incredibly worthwhile! The more you know about the marketing and planning aspects of your book writing, the more time you will save and the more money you will make! Taking a little time in the beginning to consider these valuable concepts will help you plant the *million dollar seed* of your book and set the stage for your business growth.

It is also important to hire a really good coach and mentor as it is a great idea to have that built-in sense of support in our lives—Particularly when it comes to breaking free of old paradigms and beliefs while transforming into being a new you. A lot of people will choose a coach and/or mentor for a number of different reasons. However, I have found those whom specifically speak to growth in a certain area of our lives to be the most worthwhile.

Many of the great leaders in our world have openly recognized the value and tremendous benefits of having a mentor. As one who loves to learn, I too have had many mentors during my lifetime. I have also paid close attention to *how* a mentor teaches, in addition to the pearls of wisdom that have been shared within their scope of work with me. I then take all that I have learned to my work, clients and life.

The ripple effect then is experienced by my clients during our mentoring process where they, too, feel more confident in owning their own value. They can stem from that powerful mindset of self-worth as a mentor. We create and develop their products and fee structures, which catapult the clients into earning more right out of the gate.

When I look back at being nineteen, I knew so little about the impact and ground work that would be laid for me by working with the Nordstrom brothers while launching their first store in Southern California. Although it was very intimidating at first, I learned very quickly that surrounding myself with people who knew more than me were the kind of people I wanted to be around! I remember standing at the top of the escalators with Mr. Jim Nordstrom and experiencing his excitement as the doors opened in a new location for the first time. Hearing the buzz of the crowd exploding through those doors and up the escalators was by far one of the most amazing sounds I have ever heard.

In the five years I worked there, the company opened sixty-five stores nationwide. I was there and witnessed many milestones such as the day our South Coast Plaza store reached its goal of breaking through its first one hundred thousand dollars. What I learned in those five years in terms of sales, marketing, public speaking, promotional events, and how to provide good quality service is truly beyond measure. In those five years I personally addressed five hundred organizations, groups and companies as well as maintained a clientele of about a thousand customers. I was always amazed at how people would follow me back to shop after speaking for their group because they had never heard of a Nordstrom store!

By the time I met Michael Hutchison, (aka Hutch) who had been the former VP of sales and marketing for Tony Robbins, I was more than eager to learn as much as I could about marketing as it related to the literary world. Hutch was brilliant as he helped support me with innovative ideas and concepts after my book was picked up by Random House. He instilled in me the importance of many vital aspects of marketing that I still use in my everyday work with clients.

I feel blessed to have had some amazing mentors throughout the years including the late Dottie Walters, who authored *Speak and Grow Rich.* She, in turn, was the one who introduced me to some of today's iconic authors and speakers who are included in my list of go-to experts for my clients regarding a number of different needs.

Mentoring took on a whole new meaning for me with David Neagle who is known as The Million Dollar Income Acceleration Mentor. I found it fascinating as I listened to him during our sessions. I realized David had clearly defined my abilities and gave them significant meaning.

In his discussions around money and wealth, he shared that just because we can't see it doesn't mean it doesn't exit. I am far more aware of what I have done in my own life. I realize *now* that in my mind I had seen myself healed the day I received the cancer diagnosis. I also became a published author before I finished the third rewrite, the coach for writers and authors before my book was published, and I was an opera singer receiving standing ovations while studying under Betty.

I love his extraordinary way of explaining things in very simple terms. I echo the idea that everything we desire already exists! Without knowing, I had stepped into my vision of feeling, living and being the person I wanted to be long before I reached those milestones.

I share my accomplishments with you not to blow my own horn but to hold space for you in order to live more life and achieve *your* heart's desires and dreams. Frankly, my realization fills my heart with tremendous gratitude and humility for being alive and able to make a contribution. Who do you need to be in regards to what you want?

Have you ever written a list of the things you have achieved in your life? Were you aware of who you had to be to reach your accomplishments? I believe we tend to forget or overlook the power and potential within us. I also believe it is vital to give ourselves the permission to further explore our own brilliance and the magnificence we were all given as our birth right.

What do you really want in your life? What will stop you from having what you want? As I have learned from my own mentorship, knowing the very thing that stopped me allowed me to break free of that pattern. I now recognize it before I get to the stop, and I just blow past it.

So you might ask, "What does this all have to do with writing a book or planting my *million dollar seed*? There are three points I'd like to make here. The first being that possibilities and opportunities open up to us with the mindset to receive them. The second is that having a coach or mentor can make all the difference in your growth--and the third is that asking yourself who you need to be, will help you get to the next level.

Getting out of our own way is crucial to moving forward by preventing those old patterns from stopping us from attaining our goals be it personal, professional or both. The real discipline comes in staying in that feeling as opposed to focusing on what we don't want, which is the job of the mind to keep us safe and stuck! The secret to taking every *no* and converting it into countless *yeses* is to stay intensely focused on your vision and embrace the feeling of being your desired self or outcome.

For example, asking my former husband to take care of all the calls that came as a result of my diagnosis allowed me to change my environment. I didn't know it at the time, but that was one of the best things I ever did. Though people don't often realize it, conversations that focus on the problem or story are usually what keep others stuck in it.

I had experienced a few conversations where people were already expecting me to die! Though they meant well, those conversations—if allowed to continue—would have sucked the life right out of me. This was the furthest thing from my focus in gaining more life. I even wrote a chapter on how to support someone who is recovering from cancer in *In Honor of Women* for that very reason.

Though I really didn't have the *how*, the things I needed to do showed up in a very powerful way for me. It's amazing the strength that comes when you know nothing can stop you from getting what you want and where you want to go! Interviewing oncologists before hiring one was another very interesting experience because apparently not many people do that! People would look at me as if I had three heads when I used to say, "Well, don't you meet your mechanic before he works on your car?" Finding the doctor that had the right mindset for me was an absolute must in order to keep myself focused on living life. I had to stay crystal clear on bringing in as many people and things that excited me in order to get to the next level of joy.

Writing your book as *The Million Dollar Seed* suggests a wonderful way to approach what you really want in your life—that is, of course, if your excitement is to write a book. Regardless of your skillset or what you feel you may lack, it is incredibly beneficial to start with your end goal in mind. This will naturally transform you into knowing what actions are right for you to take you to your next step.

That said, I find it very exciting to help writers and authors accelerate their growth almost immediately by sharing nine steps that cultivate many businesses. Ideally and as I have mentioned before, I love to engage in conversations regarding these steps before experts write their books. It primarily saves them time, avoids rewrites and most importantly injects a powerful marketing strategy that will position them for financial success. Hence the reason I am sharing them here. Whether you are an aspiring or already published author, these steps will help you accelerate your journey toward becoming a powerful and successful expert authority.

It is rather important to mention that the following steps are thoughtfully and intentionally placed in a consecutive fashion for the simple reason that I have found them to work best this way. Though there is much to be said about the planning that goes into a book, this is certainly a sound starting point and one that has worked beautifully for many authors.

The 9 Steps to Planting Your Book as The Million Dollar Seed…Before You Begin to Write!

1. Identify Your Target Market, Their Needs and Where to Find Them:

   Knowing this information inside and out will serve you beyond measure! This is the location where you will plant your seed as it is critical for your book's growth! One of the most monumental things you can do is to connect and build relationships with as many people (online or otherwise) whom either lead or belong to large groups, companies, and organizations that need what you have to offer!

   Once you know your market well, look for one or more bestselling authors within that field to endorse your book or write your foreword (more info on endorsements and forewords to come!). This will also offer you more credibility regarding your contents as well as potentially land nicely with traditional publishers whom may want to pick your title up later. If you contact your authors at this stage, you are more likely to have your endorsements in time for your publication rather than waiting until you're ready to go to print.

2. Identify and Create Lists:

List shortcuts, solutions, and cutting-edge ideas as important takeaways that will save your market time and money while offering your readers inspiration, knowledge, and peace of mind. These lists need to be comprised of odd numbers, (3, 5, 7, 9, and 101) as they are the standard and most recognized numbers in the literary world of how-to's and self-help books.

Remember it's all about your audience and identifying how many benefits you can offer them. Create these as part of your individual chapters that can grow into several articles for topic related magazines, blogs, individual eBooks, downloads, and interview topics. Start to use one of them as a free download offer for the opt-in feature on your website to grow your database. You know you have a great book when every chapter can potentially be a separate book. These chapters and concepts are some of the roots that will begin to grow from your book!

3. Create a Title:

Take the time to choose a brandable and memorable title (including subtitle) that speaks directly to your market; also choose one that can grow into other products and services. Your title is the foundation for your seed to grow and is what will house your empire.

4. Determine if Your Book Can Be A Series:

Take that title and create the subtitles to help brand a series much like The Chicken Soup for The Soul Series co-authored by Mark Victor Hansen and Jack Canfield, which became a huge success as a multifaceted series of books and products for a multitude of target markets. Typically, each book that is part of a series has its own audience. Your series is also part of the roots that grow from your book and will lodge itself deeply into a variety of markets, which in turn makes it easy for people to identify with your brand.

Remember to go to copyright.gov to register your title and potential series title just as soon as you have them. Something else that is important with titles, is to make sure to check on amazon and Google that your working title has not already been published!

5. Identify Your Skillset and Platform:

Create a plan on how you want to address the needs of your market using your skillset and platform. What skills and platform do you want to use to best reach your audience? This needs to include a variety of angles, revenue streams for sales, and online marketing strategies. For example, if you are a speaker who loves to talk and feels confident in selling your upcoming book and products in the back of the room, then finding a booking agent who can get you paid for your talks will help you with your plan.

You can work on getting your One-Sheet ready for your agent before or while you are writing your book. Having someone represent you is a smart way to use your time doing what you love to do—while someone else books you to speak to your target market! Knowing your platform is key. It creates the perfect environment for that seed to help you quantum leap your business.

6. Create a Business and Marketing Plan:

When you create your business and marketing plan, be sure to include specific timelines for pub dates, campaign launches, as well as your revenue goals for your products and potential services starting with the first book title. Depending on your overall time frame, you may also want to do the same for each title of the series. This plan needs to include online marketing and potential blog tours based on your preference. Here is where you can plan and forecast what you want to earn in your first year for starters. From a financial perspective, it's important to map out where you are and where you want to go! What's the income you desire? What is that magical number?

Include your other products and services within the content of your book to share with your current market. There are two reasons this will benefit your efforts enormously. The first reason is to expand your market's awareness about what products and services you offer, as well as to include other miscellaneous products that can later be used as part of your brand. There is more to come on this point as I further explain this step within this chapter. The second reason is to naturally increase your web traffic—and most importantly sales—by including your direct link to those products. Plan realistically as much as you can! Keep in mind, your plan is the water that will give your book life!

7. Create a Focus Group:

Identify a small professional focus group that is currently part of your target market or clients and/or customers, to test your ideas. Be sure to have them each sign a non-disclosure agreement to protect your intellectual property. Your focus group, which should always represent your market, is a critical aspect of where you plant your book as your seed. It is what will continue to nurture its development! For example, if your book speaks to how to effectively raise children, you would definitely want parents on your focus group as opposed to people who don't have children. The specific age group of the children your book references may also be an important factor based on what you want to achieve as your end goal.

8. Joint Ventures:

Whenever possible include seemingly miscellaneous products that will help you align with large corporations and companies that may be interested in joint venturing with you in the future.

For example, if your book is about child safety and you include the general idea and importance of car seats, you may be able to align with several car seat manufacturers and companies speaking to that topic. Your book, or that section of your book, can be offered to them as a special edition manual or booklet for their company to give-away to their customers. These inserted ideas are also what create some of the deepest roots for your business!

9. Explore and Identify Income Opportunities:

Plan ahead and begin whenever possible to incorporate your book concepts in ways that will give you cash flow as you write your material. Some of the ways to incorporate your concepts is by providing coaching/consulting services, teleseminars or workshops, and classes. This gives you an opportunity to work directly with your market and test your concepts with them, as well as build your database.

Planning and creating a stream of income is ideally key before you begin to write your manuscript. This will serve with your budget building and later costs for editing, cover design and layout. Here is where you will begin to see signs of green that is breaking ground! You are on your way to growing your empire!

The purpose of this list is to offer you some insight on the importance of having a plan. Working with a mentor and or coach before you write your book will save you insurmountable time and money in the months and years to come! As a specialist in the area of organizing an individual's work of knowledge, I am always listening for ways to format or structure key points for writers and authors. Because we live in a world of so much information, we want to offer material that cuts to the chase and is easily understood by the audience at large.

As you will have noticed, each of the nine steps is tied to the metaphor of planting a seed as specified in the title of this chapter. It was done with intention to demonstrate more substance and meaning to the concept behind this particular body of work. It is important to tie things together so you can ensure a nice, even flow of content. Personally, I love it when it flows comfortably for both the author and the reader.

For all intents and purposes, I am going to speak to some of the points related to the listed nine steps. My points will not necessarily flow in the same order as I have listed the steps.

In my reference to the second of these nine steps that speaks to identifying and creating an odd-numbered list of shortcuts, solutions, and cutting-edge ideas, I provide an example of what *my* list looks like! Though you can create and build a list for a variety of reasons, the point that I'm making is to make sure it is effective and sound in approach. In this case, each step is positioned and designed to build a book into a business and empire.

As part of the accelcration method to my work, studying each of these steps will prepare you on how to approach your book with a whole new mindset for being a successful author. Giving yourself structure will certainly ease you into the position you want for yourself.

I smile as I think of my conversation with my dear friend John Kremer, author of *1001 Ways to Market Your Books: For Authors and Publishers.* For years he has been my go-to title and book promotions expert for my clients. When it comes to creating just the right title that will best serve them and their markets, he's the man.

Together we will often do conference calls with the author on board, which gives them the best of both worlds. John will start gathering and combining key words to create a title and subtitle. I, on the other hand will keep in the forefront what the author wants to achieve within the content, marketing strategies and their skillset.

I personally had a blast creating the title for this work with him as we went back and forth on all kinds of ideas. Clearly, this very chapter would never have come into existence without the title to the book. It resonated very strongly with me the moment I heard it. I fell in love with the idea of planting a seed because it absolutely spoke to what I do for my first time writers, as well as authors and professionals. I knew it was the right title, as a whole series of products started to flood my mind!

John states, "Most authors should spend some time developing their title so it is memorable and brandable." I couldn't agree more with him because the title sets the stage–for not only the content of the book but also for the branding that takes precedence as part of launching other products and services. His website www.booktitlecritiques.com is a wonderful reference for writers and authors who need some assistance in creating a bestselling title.

The Million Dollar Seed is planned as a series. The title will grow with a variety of products and programs, two of which are already in the queue: *The Book Writing Acceleration Program* and *The Book Marketing Acceleration Program.* In addition to the programs, it is a good foundation for my Book Writing and Marketing Acceleration VIP Days for clients who want more in less time.

One of the best ways to stay connected with me is to visit www.stellatogo.com and opt-in so you can be placed on my mailing list for updates and launches of upcoming products and services. It's wonderful to be able to offer more in the ways of products, services and doing what I teach!

Like John, I have had the privilege of working with top professionals in the wonderful world of books and products that speak to authors and speakers. Over the years I made it a point to connect with authentic professionals to whom I could confidently refer clients. I have been blessed to work with these top leading experts as they give pulse to many aspects of a book.

It has been really important for me to make it as easy as possible for writers and authors to have most anything they need for their next level. My greatest motivation is remembering how challenging it was when I initially got started as a first-time writer. They are often surprised as to all that needs to come together prior and during the publication process. The reason it is so imperative to plan it all out and create timelines for each component is it helps avoid feelings of overwhelm, frustration and disappointment.

The Three Elements:

In addition to the nine steps, there are three specific elements that are a must when it comes to your *million dollar seed*!

The First Element is one of the most important foundations for planting your *million dollar seed*: your cover design. I define it as a foundation because it is meant to set the tone, as well as feel and brand specifically for *your* audience. I can't tell you how often I will see a cover that looks homemade or designed by an amateur. I am often surprised by how many writers and authors will place little value on the first thing people will see as a representation of their work. Needless to say, your cover needs to sell itself to your market. It needs to say to the person who picks it up, "Buy me. You have to have me!"

There are many authors who will have a friend, spouse or other non-professional graphic designer actually design the cover for them. You wouldn't go to a friend to do your brain surgery if he was still in med school, so don't go to an artist because they can draw or paint well. They may be very successful in their own right, but unless all they work on everyday are book covers and brand logos you really don't want to even consider them as an option.

The same goes for any professional you may hire as part of your process of becoming a successful business owner, writer, author, speaker or coach. Hiring individuals who live and breathe their work with passion and who come from a place of experience that led them to their own success is the kind of professionalism you want!

I know it can get sticky sometimes, especially when it's a spouse who happens to be an artist. I had it happen a couple of years ago where a spouse created a logo for the author that to the professional world of graphic designers would be far less than tolerated. I finally had to tell my client that his logo was viewed as inappropriate by several professionals regarding what he wanted to achieve as a leading expert in his field.

I recognize how delicate these things can be at times, but frankly this is business and it is something that merits the upmost level of professionalism. My integrity wouldn't allow me to overlook an inappropriate logo design, especially after all of his hard work on his book.

The fourth of the nine steps listed speaks to creating a series with your title that allows an author to address a number of different markets and needs. When you have a series in mind, it is imperative to hire a great cover designer who can start with the thought of creating a brandable look that will carry on to the other books and products within your series.

This design is crucial for building your brand so people will begin to identify your ownable look every time they see it because it will be recognized as unique to you. A good gauge is to ask who they've designed covers for or how long they've been designing covers as well as branding logos. Although

I am approached by many designers, my primary go-to cover and logo designers have several decades under their belts.

Depending on whether an author wants to be a bestseller will help me decide where to direct him or her. Someone who wants to position themselves as a bestseller will require sending them to my designer who is known for creating bestsellers. It's not to say that those who are not interested in being bestsellers get the raw end of the stick. They are very pleased with their covers. It simply costs less than the other.

The Second Element is the interior design of the book that needs to flow with the cover design. The feel and look needs to have consistency, and this is something many authors tend to overlook or take for granted. Certain aspects of the cover design need to be reflected within the interior, such as the feel of the font type selected for the chapter headings. As a writer or author, you should know there are a number of reasons why readers are more likely to stop reading a book and walk away from it. Knowing some of these distinctions will help you keep your audience reading!

The most common reasons people stop reading books are the obvious ones; the material doesn't flow well, is arid and simply does not hold the interest of the reader. However, there are many more reasons that also deserve attention such as the font type and size as well as the length of each paragraph. If the paragraphs are too long, it makes it harder for the reader to stay focused! Try reading a page without paragraph breaks verses one that has several breaks.

You'll probably find it easier to read the section with the breaks quickly and want to continue to the next page. A professional editor usually will catch where those paragraph breaks need to take place long before the book goes to an interior designer.

On the other hand, a professional book interior designer will automatically aim to achieve how to best layout the material so it is appealing to the eye. A trained book interior designer will take note if something is out of balance and point those things out to you. They will spend hours making sure there is consistency with spacing, as well as ensure the proper placement of graphics, quotes, illustrations, etc. Personally, I am so grateful for those who love this work as it takes a lot of time, attention to detail, and frankly the patience of a saint!

The Third Element is the treatment of endorsements and the highlight of the author's name for the foreword on the cover, which takes us back to selecting a professional book cover designer who knows where and how to place them. The placement is quite important as one endorsement may contain more pertinent and descriptive words than another, which may merit being on the front cover as opposed to the back.

I separated this element because endorsements and forewords are something to hold in high regard. When I ask for an endorsement or foreword, I really think about who best suits the material I have written. I also consider if the work beautifully complements the author since there is a strong chance we have written for the same or very similar markets. I remember the day I received each and every endorsement from my five bestselling authors for *In Honor of Women*.

Honestly, I felt like the heavens blessed me every time. Just the mere fact that they took time out of their busy schedules simply to write something for me was such a great surprise. I can't express the feeling that flooded me when the fax came from Cairo with Marianne Williamson's endorsement. Had the paper not faded, I would still have the original copy!

I refer to endorsements in the first step because for most writers and authors, it is a last item, if anything, on their to-do list. However, if you can plan to send your letters out to your authors with a simple synopsis of two or three lines specifying the basis of your work and your powerful title along with a subtitle, that is primarily all you need at that time.

I am not sure where this misconception stems

from, but a lot of people seem to think that they need to write the whole book first and send it in its entirety. In the event that an author or expert authority asks you for the whole manuscript before it is published, they should expect to receive a non-disclosure agreement from you in order to protect your intellectual property.

Although it is not something that happens to most writers and authors, I did have an experience worth writing about where I sent the whole manuscript. The last thing I ever expected was that the bestselling author I sent it to not only didn't respond to my calls and emails, but had the audacity of showing up on a talk show using some of my concepts.

Now, what was interesting was that I wasn't watching TV at the time, but our phone kept ringing that night with friends calling to let us know what was happening! They knew I had been waiting for a response from her. At first I thought they were kidding, but as I tuned in I heard her languaging shift to the words specifically tailored to my work. My concepts were entirely different than her concepts, yet she clearly touched on them.

As time passed, I fell into a conversation with someone who knew this person. Honestly, I was so surprised by her behavior. More than anything I was just curious as to why someone of her caliber and national recognition would ever consider taking another author's work.

When I shared what I believed had happened, this person freely volunteered that the author had a habit of attempting to do the same with both well-known bestselling authors as well as unknown writers! What was noteworthy was that of all the individuals I asked for endorsements, she was the only one who requested to see the whole manuscript. Fortunately for me, she didn't affect my work in any way. I share this story only to help you avoid drama since there truly is no need for it in the midst of so much excitement.

While asking for an endorsement, it is often appreciated by the authors if you can give about three samples of something you would like them to say about your work. Due to their busy schedules, they will at times only select the sample they like the best while other authors will take the time to write their own.

When it comes to a foreword, it's also appreciated if we can give the author a starting point so as to speed up the process for them. It's important to make it easy for them to pick up where you left off perhaps after two or three sentences. Imagine, one day people will perhaps come to you for your endorsements and forewords. As much as I would love to give more endorsements, I especially don't if my hand is in the creation of the work in question. I personally wouldn't consider it appropriate to endorse a body of work authored by one of my clients for that reason.

The sixth step listed speaks to the importance of expanding your market's awareness about the products and services you offer, including miscellaneous products whenever possible, that you can later develop as part of your brand. As you may recall, I referred earlier to Kimberlee Schultz, the author of the children's seven book series, *The StarPals*™.

Right from the start, Kimberlee knew her focus was to create seven titles that were each directly linked to a particular virtue and a character named by that virtue. Anchored with *Patty Patience*, as her first book for the series, her vision included *The StarPals*™ *Treasure Chart* for children to track their good deeds with their parents, teachers and care takers. The chart, which is loved by children and adults, is a standalone product that is sold separately or with the series.

In addition to teaching children what each virtue looks like in real life as well as the value of family, friendship, philanthropy, environment, and personal achievement, we sprinkled a variety of what I call "miscellaneous products" within the series. In her case, it was imperative to get a registered trademark for her brand, which is vital for the development of her forecasted products. I fell in love with this project from day one as it is a phenomenal example of what is possible with a book concept.

The Million Dollar Seed approach of creating a series with an initial book idea right from the start made it easy for Kimberlee to bring her vision to life. Right from the beginning we went to an illustrator with the idea of producing *Patty Patience* as a template for the other six books. Having a template was a huge plus as Kimberlee knew to build nine scenarios as the structure and consistency for branding purposes for each book. We had a blast bringing some of her wonderful childhood memories back to life for children and parents to relate to!

At one point, a parent inquired if Kimberlee had dolls for sale because her little girl wanted a *Patty Patience* doll. Once her trademark was in place, it was easy to have fun coming up with a variety of different products and have the illustrator then include these items in her books.

Her brand made it easy to have fun with all kinds of product ideas. So, off we were to the races! Kimberlee and I worked with the illustrator to include dolls, puppets, a board game, flash cards, aprons and more within the series. The *I am a StarPal*™ accountability button featured in several of her books, was a fantastic add on and one that is a "must have" for the children whom are part of the StarPal's™ Social Emotional Empowerment Development (SEED) Platform—being offered in elementary schools in Southern California.

Kimberlee has also developed certificates for

the children, and she will continue to bring more of her illustrated products to life as her business soars! *The StarPals™ Series* is a great representation of *The Million Dollar Seed*. Not only is the concept simple, but children really love these books as they have fun learning while being empowered and rewarded for good behavior. When I look at the positive impact this series is having on children, their families and schools, it is easy to see that Kimberlee's timeless books will continue to be successful for many generations!

It is also exciting to look for opportunities that can appear with an extraordinary story or novel. When P. A. Staes came to me with her already written manuscript, she reluctantly handed it to me for fear that I would think it was either written poorly or that the story itself didn't merit any accolades. From the moment I started reading it, I discovered it to be not only riveting in plot but definitely worth exploring the possibility of it being a blockbuster.

I called her shortly after reading more than half the novel to tell her she really had written an amazing story quite worthy of not only being published but also becoming a movie. I felt strongly that this work would rock audiences around the world. I went on to tell her I experienced her book, *The Bruges Tapestry*, as a cross between the movie *Pride and Prejudice* and *The Da Vinci Code*. Although P. A. refers to her work as a historical mystery, I absolutely was taken by the subtle, yet beautifully intertwined romance story within it.

In my world, it is rare to find a body of work that requires very little, if any, effort. *The Bruges Tapestry* is the type of novel that takes you in and doesn't let go until you finish it! I am so thrilled for her as I have introduced her to a professional screenplay writer/film producer from Hollywood who really wants the project.

If you have written a novel or are in the process of writing a really great story, know that it may be worth your while to have someone review it. Remember to carry your non-disclosure agreements with you and to not discuss important aspects of your work with anyone less than professional unless your manuscript is published!

It is my understanding that Hollywood purchases screenplays primarily from the month of March until September. Once again, it is important to interview a few screenplay writers before you find the one that best meets your needs. I like to refer to screenplay writers who are well connected in the industry.

Regardless of the type of *million dollar seed* you plant, be it for children, hopeless romantics, or the business world, surround yourself with as many people as possible willing to raise you to the top!

More than anything else share your vision, passion and concepts wisely with your audiences so you can be paid well for your efficiency. Build your empire with confidence and know that your fingerprint is unlike any other! Find new meaning in being the author of your life while creating wealth and living your dream!

"Motivation naturally evolves from intention but to be motivated without intention seems like a backwards approach and one that is harder to achieve!"

– Stella Togo

CHAPTER 5

FRAME YOUR BOOK WITH THE 7 INTENTIONS

I recently met Miranda Mary, an adorable bright-eyed little girl who completely surprised me with her writing! In less than two months she had already completed authoring about twenty little books before turning seven. She is very gifted as she is also her own illustrator. I had never met a child author particularly at her age with a greater sense of intentionality for her work.

There she was sitting in the oversized office chair next to me in her father's conference room when we met for the first time to discuss her books. Her face lit up as she showed me some of her favorite books and read them aloud to me.

Now, what was funny was how she caught an occasional word like *tree* that was supposed to be *three* and said, "Oh! That's wrong. I wrote that when I was little!"

I laughed and looked at her parents and said, "Didn't she write this just a few months ago?" They laughed while nodding yes, confirming my understanding. I later learned that she refers to me as "My Miss Stella", which *just* melts me.

Not only did Miranda Mary use a different theme that was carried out throughout each book, some books even had messages within their stories. In addition to writing *with* intention, she also was crystal clear as to the intent of her books.

She in fact said she wanted to help other children write their stories. Unlike most people, Miranda spoke as if she had been an author for many years! In a very matter of fact way, she referred to her work as *my books.* I was absolutely marveled by her outstanding level of confidence and ownership. It certainly isn't something I see every day, especially with children.

With her remarkable school teacher by her side, Miranda Mary's enthusiasm became contagious while she inspired her classmates to also write like her. Hence the name and title of her series, *Miranda Mary's Write Like Me Series* ™—an extraordinary concept. It holds tremendous potential for many other products and programs. The mind boggles at all of the prosperous possibilities!

In prior pages, I have shown you the importance of marketing with intention, which of course naturally moves right into writing with intention. It is the intention behind the marketing that frequently feeds writers with passion leading the book to practically write itself. What do I mean by that?

It will most likely ignite you at your very core when you know whom you are writing for, how to reach them and what you have to offer them. All that is left is to let your passion write for you as you prioritize and add structure to your content. The comment I usually hear that's music to my ears is, "I never thought writing a book could be so easy!"

Having the component of structure in place simply requires prioritizing your thoughts and the importance of the material in question. Usually writers will voice their content in a very methodical or chronological order within minutes based on some very poignant questions I ask them during our first session. Follow your gut on what sounds and feels right to you in terms of the order or sequence of chapters for your books.

Although unfamiliar to most writers, there are certain things that will stop them. Writer's block is difficult for those who experience it. However, I honestly believe it is fundamentally impossible to experience one when you're writing from the accelerated approach and intention of *The Million Dollar Seed*. In all of my years of speaking with writers and authors, I can think of two individuals who came to me with this experience prior to working together. I have spoken with many writers whom have plainly stopped writing for quite some time. In some cases they never go back to their writing as a result.

I want to speak to this issue as it is something that can get in the way for writers. Perhaps I can shed some light where it may be needed. Though I am not a psychologist, what I have found is that writer's block is at times linked to childhood trauma. For example, a strict parent or caretaker may have unknowingly emotionally scarred someone at a young age.

While reflecting on one of the individuals whom had experienced the block, I recall asking him if he was open to breaking free of it. As he responded with excitement at the possibility of writing again, I allowed my curiosity to take the lead because it has never misled me.

I found it interesting that he had stopped writing following a certain visit with his mother. This particular visit had taken place about six years prior to meeting him.

After a short series of questions, I discovered his mother had been an English teacher and scholar for many years. He recounted how she had scolded him countless times as a child. Apparently, this happened quite frequently while doing his homework.

Her comments to him as an adult about being a writer and potential author subconsciously took him back to those childhood experiences. Without ever thinking about that conversation again, he at the time didn't realize her words immediately stopped him in his tracks.

He essentially didn't write for an entire six years, but he couldn't understand why he was unable to get back into it. He spoke of his frustration that haunted him because he truly enjoyed expressing himself through his writing.

His face totally lit up once he realized the connection, and he was immediately able to release the block within our brief conversation. It took him all but a minute to fully see that her opinion was *just* an opinion.

He soon asserted he didn't have to own that opinion anymore nor had to feel the way he had as a child for so many years. In his heart, he knew he had been a good writer. He spoke of how his friends had repeatedly supported that facet of his life. I was so happy to know he started writing again.

I smile when I think of all the times I got yelled at for waking up really early on a Saturday morning to read my second grade books. I missed out on a lot of the popular Saturday morning cartoons and TV shows. They didn't seem to matter as I remember being so fascinated by stories. Looking back I'm grateful my mother didn't succeed in halting my passion for books. In fact, I think she probably propelled it!

One of the most passionate professionals I have ever worked with is Erick Debanff, a respiratory therapist of a combined forty-five years of experience and one who revitalizes the spirit of any one who crosses his path.

We use the term *combined* for his experience because for years he has worked full time both a graveyard and regular shift. What completely blew me away with Erick was his determination to live life to the fullest and teach others through example.

He spoke of how he would run up and down several flights of stairs to stay awake during the night hours instead of drinking coffee! I couldn't believe my ears as he told me he only required two hours of sleep every day. I think I actually had him repeat himself because my mind couldn't register how that was possible.

From the moment I first spoke with him, I recognized the incomparable value he would offer the masses with a book. As the author of *Vie Max: How to Live Your Next 2 Billion Heartbeats to the Max*, Erick Debanff shares some of the most riveting true life stories and accounts that make my heart soar with joy, appreciation and gratitude for being alive!

I remember the times I would be moved to tears as I read his stories prior to our coaching session. I was fascinated by how much passion was exhibited in his writing about his world travels as well as the veil between life and death that propelled his desire to always do more!

It was astonishing to learn how he unknowingly used quantum physics and the power of intention to help a critically hospitalized young girl dramatically increase her breathing capability—while at the time hiking on a mountain top with great speed!

Every story shared in his book is written with the intention of invigorating the spirit of every reader and person who hears him speak at any live event.

His audiences are usually completely spellbound! Though many would like to refer to him as a motivational speaker, they realize pretty quickly that Erick's message goes far deeper as it is based on getting results through intentionality instead of motivation.

To me, motivation naturally evolves from intention but to be motivated without intention seems like a backwards approach and one that would be harder to achieve! For example, I could say I have been motivated to offer this content for a while.

However, setting the intention to launch and offer it at an upcoming event gives new meaning to my initial motivation.

My intention immediately became a commitment which led me to metaphorically move mountains—as I have been writing until 3am and waking up at 8am to efficiently work with my clients.

I do believe that most people approach book writing with good intentions. However, the intentions I want to elaborate on are the kind that lay the groundwork and structure for your exciting concepts to immediately take flight!

The 7 Intentions

Intention #1: For Creating Your Environment

As a professional writer, I believe it is important to set the stage for your writing because it will help you stay focused and accomplish more in less time. One of the things I would like to suggest to you is to set time aside in your mind as to when to do your work.

Once you have that intention, the mind has a wonderful way of making sure you have many of your thoughts ready to go! You may be amazed as to how much thought comes pouring out of you by the time you get to your computer. It never ceases to amaze me as to how well that works!

Although everyone is a little different, I will usually suggest they create a space to work that is just for them if they don't already have one. It needs to be quiet and clear of distractions whenever possible!

For example, within my space I like to have fresh flowers to look at as I ponder my thoughts. I like to have a special lighting as well as instrumental or a meditative type of background music. This feeds my inspiration for feelings that result in words. Sometimes, I will light a candle or use my fireplace to give me the cozy feeling I want to give my readers depending on what I want to convey or express to them at that moment.

Although it is obvious that your work is for your readers, I believe it's important to declare this time for writing as your own. As I have mentioned before, we tend to write the books that teach us the most!

Recognize that this is your time for reflection and personal growth as well as potentially for your reader. One of the nicest things about this process many refer to as therapeutic is that things are beautifully revealed to us that we normally wouldn't have seen otherwise.

The development of content flow requires contemplation and a quiet space to hear your thoughts along with your heart. Remember to write from a peaceful place for your reader. A peaceful environment within your mind, as well as the one you are sitting in, will bring forth or convey that type of feeling for your audience.

As I write, I am reminded of a particular writer whom made me aware of the writer's state of mind while expressing thoughts on paper. At first I was a little confused as to the flow of her content until I realized what she had given me must had been written at different times in her life—possibly years apart.

She laughed when I asked her if in fact my suspicions were correct. She revealed that in fact she had started writing years ago and had recently picked it up again. When asked how I knew, I told her the person who wrote the last insertion was far more self-realized than the person who initially began the project.

I went on to explain that her voice in the earlier pages from her prior years reflected anger and discomfort as opposed to the evolved peaceful voice that was spectacularly expressed in the later pages! She was really surprised to know that I could feel and experience the difference. Well, I find that most readers can feel more than one may think!

There was also another woman who was in the process of writing her personal account featuring her painful experiences with her mother. At one point I realized that the particular chapter we were working on stirred up lots of emotion for her and was being written from an angry place.

Knowing and believing she would be in a completely contrasting place in her mind by the time we would get to her last chapter, I suggested we skip that one for the time being.

Referring back to my experience with others, I felt the rest of the book would help her develop a sense of peace. I knew that coming back to that chapter with fresh eyes would be a much healthier approach for her. I further explained the benefits to this methodology for her and her readers so she agreed to keep moving forward.

When we came back to that section, she acknowledged the difference in her feelings between the present and how she felt just a few months prior! This time around she had already forgiven her mother and could now write from that experience without having to relive the other experiences.

She no longer had to feel all of the negative emotions that could have kept her stuck in the drama of it all, which could have certainly stopped her from continuing to write her book all together. She was able to see the advantage of clear expression that came from her healthier sense of self, and this provided her readers to experience the same thing.

Be aware that your environment begins in your mind and then is reflected to that which is around you. I often tell writers to be gentle with themselves and to choose a path that works best for them and the project at hand. Every now and then it is nice to get away to a place that gives you a sense of feeling renewed, which can also strengthen your sense of peace.

I have been known to take myself on a trip for the sake of changing my physical environment so that I can completely dedicate myself to my readers. I typically have my food delivered to me to make sure I take care of myself as I rest in between my hours of work. Most of all it is my intention and mindset to stay clear of *any* interference. It's funny but my readers own me when I write for them! Creating a comfortable and beautiful environment makes for not only good writing but provides both you and your audience the full experience of gratification.

Create a beautiful place in your mind that is free and at peace, as well as create a comfortable space that allows your creative genius to come to life with your words.

Intention #2: For Your Book Dedication

A dedication in a book speaks volumes to whom is important to you. Although it can be a special entry for authors, many overlook this part of their book. Regardless of the type or genre of book, I feel it is a wonderful thing to dedicate your work to a special person or people significant in your life. It's usually viewed as an exceptional acknowledgement.

Chances are your books and dedications will be around for many decades, which may be something that also has a positive impact on your future family generations.

Set the intention for writing a timeless and beautiful dedication for the significant person or people in your life.

Intention #3: For Your Acknowledgements

Acknowledging the individuals that have supported your growth, desires and dreams is also a wonderful and significant aspect of your book. When acknowledging someone in writing, recognize that person as though you were speaking to them so they can read the personal feeling behind the words.

A lot of authors will acknowledge an individual in third person but doing it in first is more meaningful. I encourage people to put feeling into this section of their book. I learned a long time ago that public acknowledgements can be worthwhile, especially when they come from the heart.

Set the intention to wholeheartedly and personally thank those who have supported and loved you throughout your life journey or writing process.

Intention #4: For Your Table of Contents

Your table of contents should include the headings of your chapters in a methodical format according to the importance or priority of the information.

One of the greatest mistakes writers and authors make is to save the best chapter for last causing them to unknowingly risk losing their reader at the midway point. I typically suggest in those cases starting with the best chapters and watching how the material develops itself to keep up with what is set right at the beginning.

People usually pause as they don't normally expect me to restructure their work, however who wants to wait to get to the good stuff at the end of a book when it can be present not only at the beginning but also throughout the book? I often will say, "Think of yourself as the reader. Wouldn't it be exciting to learn this in the opening pages?"

One of the biggest concerns I hear all the time is, "Do I have enough information for a two hundred plus page book? If I start with my best stuff first, I might run out of information to write about!"

The mind is a funny thing to me. Most people have an accumulation of years of knowledge and experience that is beyond comprehension. Some even have several lifetimes worth of stories depending on their background and understanding.

In my experience, I have not found anyone whom runs out of thoughts for a book within just a few pages. For example, writing an eBook naturally sets the tone for considerably fewer pages, but that is clearly intended for this type of book. However, I have never seen a lack of knowledge or writing potential for material with anyone.

In fact, it's always fun to hear the amazement when an author who feared not having enough information finds themselves reaching what they considered to be a milestone of a secretly held number of pages. They usually laugh as they announce their personal milestone and very quickly realize how unrealistic that fear was for them.

As you identify the most important and pertinent benefits, solutions or flow of contents for your reader, don't worry about word or page count because those things will take care of themselves. I'd rather see someone place their energy on providing the greatest value within the content of each chapter rather than their word or page count any day!

Believe me when I say that your reader doesn't care about your word or page count, especially if what you have to offer can rock their world!

With the proper layout of your thoughts for each chapter, consider titles that directly speak to the content. A good guideline in building your content is to identify great chapter headings that can potentially be a standalone eBook or developed into another product.

Set the intention to create strong sought-after chapter headings that directly speak to their individually rich content, book title and market.

Intention #5: For Your Introduction

Many of you have heard me say countless times that an introduction should be the *very* last thing you write because you will know all that your book contains when you are completely done writing it—not a moment before! This approach will save you more time than you can imagine!

When you reach the last word of your final chapter, you can take a few days, to reflect all that you have shared and to set the tone for your readers. This section of the book needs to be concise and to the point. A lot of people like to read introductions because it gives them a feel as to the author's intention for them.

The introduction is where you whet the appetite of your readers and give them something to look forward to! The nice thing about doing it at the end is that it is easier to be brief because by then you have gotten all of the writing out of your system. Your level of confidence with the accomplishment of completing your book will make you write from an entirely different place. For most authors, writing your introduction at the end is like the cherry on top of an ice cream sundae!

Set the intention to whet your audience's appetite and give them a sneak preview of what's in store!

Intention #6: For Your Chapters

Each and every chapter needs to build onto the next with specific points, along with stories and personal reflections that cement those points for your readers. Make it easy for them to understand by saying what you really want to say, and in a way that is to the point! Help them laser their thinking so as to be clear on what you are offering them at all times.

Write to and for your audience with the intention that your information, based on your research, will be of great benefit and service to them. Believe in yourself and what you have to offer! As you do so, hold the space for your recipients to appreciate your knowledge and insight. It's virtually impossible to intend for their best interest while not writing from the heart. Readers will relate to you more when you place more of you into your words, chapters and book.

Avoid being overwhelmed by identifying and choosing three to five specific points you wish to make for each chapter prior to sitting down and writing them. Once you have your points of reference established it is much easier to address each one with stories, steps or tools that best convey your expression.

Set the intention that the three to five points you will cover in each chapter will benefit the most people within your market.

Intention #7: For Your Finishing Touches

Once you have all of your different parts in place (e.g. dedication, acknowledgements, introduction, table of contents) and your content is written, it is time to add the finishing touches to frame your work—especially if it is a how-to, self-help, manual or memoir type of book. Much like a frame on a picture or painting, there are certain things that help bring out the colors in your book.

These items include special quotes, testimonials, poems, illustrations, graphs, opening and closing thoughts or prayers, cartoons, and anything that can be considered an accessory to your work. However, it is essential to not clutter your book as it may take away from the flow of the contents.

I usually will suggest giving these items a special treatment by placing them on a separate page whenever possible. For example, you can choose to open every chapter with a quote that speaks either to the chapter itself or the overall message of the book that loops itself back to the title.

If you wish to highlight the quote and give it its own page, you will need to place it on the left page opposite the text or at the beginning of the next chapter on the right page. It is always a wonderful idea to frame each chapter with a quote, poem or some of the other items I have listed. A quote will often set the intention for what the reader will learn in that next chapter.

It's fun to include some of your own quotes if you have cultivated some that would tie into your work. Remember they need to be pertinent to your topic. I laugh as I think of being on the phone with a client that may say something that sounds like a great quote during our session. I'll immediately ask them to write it down because it is usually those little pearls of wisdom that go unrecognized but can be utilized this way.

These quotes can also be used to create a collection of inspirational thoughts, which can be sold as a different product to support your brand. For example, a journal to accompany your *million dollar seed* can carry the look and feel of your cover, but you can simply add the word *journal* to the title. Now you add your inspirational quotes at the top of the blank lined pages or sections.

The same can be done with poems. I actually know a couple of people I can go to when a client needs poems for their book. Of course, like any other person you hire, it is important to have them sign an agreement so you can use their poems to frame your work. If they are given to you as a gift, then I still suggest you get an agreement. Have them sign it to cover any unknown and/or future expectations. As a side note, it is always a good idea to meet with an attorney before you enter into any agreement.

Typically a single quote, poem, or illustration to open a chapter will suffice. If you already have images or illustrations within the content, you may want to offer a quote or poem instead of an illustration just to add balance.

For example, the idea of using photos in a legacy book to open each chapter will be appreciated for many generations to come! A person who writes a legacy book will want to highlight special times in life to share with their loved ones. In some cases we actually can start with the theme of significant photos to create the chapters and feel of the book.

It's always exciting to explore what can be used as a final touch within the pages to make or give a book that special something! Don't miss out on the opportunity to add that special something to your work!

Perhaps one of the most important final touches that people often overlook is the copy on the back cover of the book! Your back cover copy is the second thing your readers will look at! Of course, your front cover is the first thing they will see. Know that what is written on the back will be the determining factor for most people. If your words speak volumes to their needs, then they will purchase your book.

It is imperative to choose your words wisely and write as efficiently as possible. Your back cover needs to offer the significance of the content. The benefits need to be worded in such a way that will make consumers want to read what's inside! This element is what ultimately frames all of your work, so make it rock for your audience!

Depending on the type of genre and of course the preference of the author, headshots or still photos can be positioned in different places. In general some books (e.g. how-to's and self-help) require the author's photo to be placed on the bottom left corner of the back cover.

Other categories like memoirs and autobiographies can have the photo of the author inside on the end pages. Some authors prefer their photo on the front cover as well. It really depends on the individual and what they want to achieve when it comes to this element.

I often will encourage authors to get a fresh and updated headshot or still photo. It is nice for readers to put a face with the voice within the pages. I laugh as I reflect on something that happened to me regarding my photo on my first book. I was getting ready to do a signing at the Fashion Island Barnes & Noble in Newport Beach, California. While I was setting up, a woman walked up to my table. What happened next really caught me by surprise.

As she picked up one of my books, she looked at the front cover and then the back. Then she asked me when the author was going to arrive. I looked at her and told her *I* was the author. This little woman looked at me as if I was speaking a different language. With her thick accent she said, "You're not the author. This is not you!" as she pointed to my photo on the back of the book.

I immediately realized my desire for being a blonde would be short lived! As a natural brunette in the photo, it really threw her off to see me as a blonde! I thought it would be fun to try something new. I completely forgot about my cover photo. Bless her heart. The funny thing is I'm not sure if she ever really believed me given the look on her face! Don't make the mistake of changing your look drastically as I did after you get published! You may want to consider keeping the same look for a while.

Another very important finishing touch is the addition of testimonials and endorsements. Testimonials are tributes usually offered by individuals who have benefited from your expertise, services or products. They can be clients or customers you may have served from the past. Their tributes are to be placed on the back cover.

The testimonials can also be positioned as the beginning pages prior to your table of contents. The words should speak to the benefits that relate directly to your title, subtitle and content. This element, when done properly, is a finishing touch that will enhance your work and offer more credibility.

Endorsements are usually written by fellow expert authors who speak to your topic and benefits as well. Prioritizing endorsements and selecting one that will go on the front cover requires consideration. You'll want to choose the strongest one that relates the most for the front cover while placing the others on the back cover.

With five bestselling author endorsements for *In Honor of Women, A Revolutionary Approach to Preventing Breast Cancer*, it was significant for me to place Marianne Williamson's on the cover for a number of reasons. She wrote, "Stella Crawley brings inspired hope into a fearful situation. May her gentle comfort reach the hearts of women everywhere." Within her beautiful words, she added inspiration while poignantly addressed the fear that many women face with the topic of breast cancer.

Although each endorsement is equally eloquent in context, Marianne truly framed my title and subtitle within her choice of words. Louise Hay wrote, "Stella Crawley's book is a beautiful testament to the courage and strength of women and to the wonder of life." This quote is also very rich. As much as I loved them all, I had to place the one that spoke to my market's emotional needs the most on the front cover.

While subtle in nature, I hope you can see the point I am making in terms of identifying the endorsement that best supports the title and subtitle. We want to make sure our audience knows that we really understand what they need or are going through. Ask yourself: if you are someone who is experiencing what the market is for you as an author, which endorsement would speak the loudest to you? That's the one you choose!

As a side note, for those of you who may be wondering, Crawley was my married name and one I have not used for many years since my divorce. However, it is important to me to honor these amazing authors by giving you their exact words and quotes.

Set the intention to frame your work with style, beauty and inspiration!

"When you publish your book you give yourself and the world a great gift!"

– Stella Togo

CHAPTER 6

GET YOUR BOOK PUBLISHED

It was shortly before I received my call from Random House that I was approached by a publisher. I had briefly met him at a networking event when he asked me to send him a copy of my self-published book. He sounded really excited on the phone as he completely showered me with accolades and kind words. Based on his specific references to my content, it appeared as though he had read it in its entirety.

Being a first time author, I was awestruck by his eagerness. I had never spoken with a publisher before, so I reveled in the joy of it all. Since my vision was to have my book picked up, I jumped at the chance to meet with him. At our meeting, I discovered some rather unusual things about his world of publishing.

What was interesting was that he wanted me to pay *him* to publish my book. I had already paid to self-publish and print several thousand copies. This was a far cry from what I had envisioned all along. However, I had to admit his enthusiasm was astonishing, and it did intrigue me. But, this is not at all what I had in mind.

I had received sixty letters of rejection by then, so this response was more than welcomed. I so badly wanted to believe what he had to say was true. But something within me said to not rush things but instead take my time. This little voice inside was beckoning me to be cautious—something didn't feel right to me. Yet, with every call, the gentleman seemed to say all the *right* things. He painted a picture regarding my marketing that made me want to look deeper into his offerings.

Fortunately, I had spoken with Mark Victor Hansen, the co-author of *The Chicken Soup Series* who had given me the name of an entertainment attorney at the time. I showed the attorney the agreement I was being asked to sign by this publisher. I'll never forget the look on the attorney's face when he told me how I would be making a huge mistake if I were to sign with this man.

I immediately called the publisher and told him I was not interested in his services. In that conversation, I realized he actually had never read my book. In fact, he was far from being honest with me. I also imagined him opening up to random pages and pulling out things to discuss with me. It frightens me to think of how different my life would've been had I not met with the attorney and instead signed straight away with the publisher. I am so glad I listened to my intuition.

The strange thing is that there are lots of people out there who prey on writers soon-to-be first-time authors. They know that writers love to be acknowledged for their work. They also prey on those whom may not have educated themselves on how to publish. This is definitely a target market you don't want to be part of!

What most people don't know is that anyone can set themselves up as a publisher. It requires very little effort to set up a publishing house: the middle company for getting an author's book on Amazon. Book writers need to be aware of these types of individuals and vanity publishing companies because they don't offer anything more than what you can do for yourself. It should be a red flag when someone wants to charge you to publish your book and take a large percentage of your profits.

Discernment is highly recommended as there may be some things listed within the fine print that can only be seen by a good intellectual rights attorney. The most crucial thing is to make sure you keep your rights. At times people want to be published so badly that they settle for anything that comes along, and usually find themselves regretting their decision later.

Sadly, I've run into many people who have fallen victim to this sort of situation. I share this experience to enlighten those of you who want someone to publish your work on your behalf. It's amazing what one meeting with an attorney can do to prevent a major disaster from happening!

Needless to say, my attorney was more than ecstatic when he learned what had happened in New York. After reviewing the paperwork, he confirmed everything was perfect and congratulated me on my success. He also confirmed that had I signed those documents, I wouldn't have been able to sell my rights as I did to Random House.

Self-Publishing verses Traditional Publishing

One of the most frequently asked questions I hear is, whether or not it is better to go into self-publishing or traditional publishing. By the way, the term *traditional* is given to publishers that will purchase your rights and usually handle your distribution. Many of these publishing companies or houses are well-known and are located in New York.

Being traditionally published is a wonderful

thing as it adds a special dynamic, sense of credential and acknowledgement to your work. Like anything else, however, you have to research and find the publishers, editors and agents that are already successful with your genre and title type.

The thing is you may need to have a lot more information before you can make an educated decision. How a writer or author chooses to publish may be one of the most important business decisions they will ever make! Some prefer the route of traditional publishing while others prefer self-publishing for a variety of reasons.

It is important to mention that you, and only you, can place the proper value onto your intellectual property. If you don't place value on it, then you can't expect someone else to give it any more worth. Once you feel you have gathered all of your information and aligned it with your ultimate desired outcome, then you are well on your way toward publishing. You will most likely make the best decision for yourself and your book.

One could potentially experience the best of both worlds when equipped with a solid, strategic plan. It really all depends on what's important to you and what is going to give you the fastest business growing results. Good questions to ask yourself include "What is going to help me get my books in the hands of my target market right away? What or who will offer me the highest paying royalties?" I encourage people to take action with a sense of urgency for the sake of their readers. Look for solutions that will enhance your experience while serving your audience sooner rather than later. Remember, they are waiting for you and your information.

The Benefits of Self-Publishing

As mentioned, creating your own publishing company and publishing your own book is one of the easiest things you can do!

The internet was nowhere near where it is today when I first self-published, *In Honor of Women,* which was later printed as a second edition with Ballantine Books. Back then, we authors really didn't have many choices other than to have copies printed through a printer.

The problem was that a lot of folks ended up with their garages being stacked with boxes. That was one of the biggest complaints I heard at the time. The other complaint was that many felt they had to handle the fulfillment side of things themselves, which was a huge hassle! Handling all of the packaging and shipping was a job in and of itself.

Things didn't really change drastically for published authors until there were dramatic technological advances in the literary industry. In fact,

Print On Demand (POD) was introduced after digital printing because it was not economical to print single copies using traditional printing technology such as letterpress and offset printing.

POD is a printing technology and business process in which new copies of a book are not printed until an order has been received, which makes it so easy to self-publish since books can be printed one at a time! Although there are many independent publishing companies that provide great services and quality products, the one that stands out the most for me and many of my clients is CreateSpace.com. This company, a sister company to Amazon, is without a doubt one of the finest on so many levels.

When it comes to extraordinary service, high royalties, and global distribution, CreateSpace is definitely the leader. When you have a question, their staff will call you the moment you hit the enter key submitting your question on your computer.

In fact, one of my clients called me with utter amazement about that very feature! The majority of my authors have used this wonderful publishing tool because it is so easy! They can order however many books they need for an event and pay much less than going to a regular printer.

For example, a two hundred page book may be sold for about twenty dollars, and an author may earn more than ten dollars in royalties per unit while keeping their rights. Now it is important to mention that things vary in cost and that this is just an instance of what is possible.

In my opinion, I think it is better to start with self-publishing for many reasons, especially with POD and the royalty factor that is available these days with CreateSpace. Based on my own experience, POD would have saved me thousands of dollars in printing costs. What was also costly was the higher quality paper I initially used to publish my book. Postage for my first edition was more expensive because the book weighed about a pound compared to a half pound with the second edition published by Ballantine Books using industry standard paper—huge difference! However, I really enjoyed getting some sales under my belt, which gave me more confidence and leverage for ultimately selling my rights.

Another benefit of self-publishing is that it gives authors an opportunity to test their market with their first edition while simultaneously sending copies to several traditional publishers. Believe me when I say there is nothing worse than sending your manuscript off to some of the large houses and getting caught up in the waiting game.

I have seen how incredibly busy professional editors who work for large houses are and how that affects the number of writers they can respond to—it really isn't personal. However, choosing to stay proactive and moving full steam ahead helps keep your momentum up! Unfortunately, a good number of manuscripts are destined to be piled up on the desks of editors, or worse, in the trash. It made me sad to see manuscripts in the trash containers under the desks, as I felt for those writers.

Personally, I think it is much easier and healthier to initially self-publish since it is so cost efficient! If a publisher eventually calls and asks you to come visit them in New York, it will be as much of a wonderful surprise for you as it was for me. At the very least you can give yourself the permission to hit the ground running, instead of holding yourself hostage while waiting for them to get back to you!

Do you know what the greatest myth in traditional publishing is? Many writers believe that once a traditional publisher picks them up, the publishers will handle all of their marketing for them. This is far from true. They may help you launch with a tour and some PR, but only for a short time. In my case, my chief editor told me that one of the main reasons they were sending me on tour was because they felt I was savvy and liked my level of confidence. She continued to say that it was a rare occurrence for them to do the same for other authors.

I really want to emphasize that traditional

publishers absolutely love authors who have a platform and are eager to sell their books. In fact, they are very interested in knowing how authors have positioned themselves. This is the reason why it is so important to start with a strong business mindset coupled with a strong set of skills. In fact, having both of these assets will offer you a greater opportunity to potentially experience the self-published route along with the traditional route.

10 Tips on How to Prepare Yourself for Self-Publishing

1. Start with your edited and polished manuscript
2. Get releases signed from all the individuals you quote in your book. You will want to do this before your book goes to print.
3. Identify the trim size for your book by measuring similar books in your field
4. Go to a book store and look at bestsellers in your genre to see what sells best in terms of size and look! This can be done online to some degree, but I find it enjoyable to see and hold the books.
5. Study what bestselling books in your category look like so as to get a feel as to how the cover design flows on to the interior pages. Notice margins and the layout of the pages.

6. Research a variety of companies that match your specific needs that can help you self-publish with POD
7. Get your photo or head shot taken by a professional photographer
8. Consider setting a publication (PUB) date for your audience and launch campaign
9. Research cover designers, layout designers, editors and proofreaders
10. Send your manuscript to the professional readers for review and feedback after receiving a non-disclosure, signed agreement

Your Publishing Support Team

Please note the word *book* is inserted in front of each professional title listed in this section (with the exception of the web designer, social media expert and photographer). There is a reason for this as these individuals are specialized in working with the needs of an author and their books.

Just as you wouldn't go to a regular doctor for your teeth, you wouldn't go to a webmaster who works with all industries. For instance, working with a web designer who is accustomed to working with authors knows how to treat the placement of a book. They will guide you on what has worked for their clients in selling their books.

Writers and authors need to seek out those who are trained in exactly what they want to achieve with their book. Take pride in your manuscript, and find the people who are going to reflect that same sense of pride in their abilities. It is monumental to work with professionals who understand the significance of how their part will enhance your book for your market.

I can't begin to tell you how much time, money and frustration you will save by taking this approach. When you choose to work with these specialists, they will know what questions to ask you that you probably would never have thought of on your own.

They know how to watch your back and are eager to build a wonderful relationship with you; they also know that if they do a good job, you're likely to write another book or do a series with them. What was so surprising for me at first was finding out many of them know each other. Chances are when you hire one of them, they will more than likely know where to send you for your other needs.

For example, when I hired my cover designer for *In Honor of Women*, she already knew of several different layout designers. I ended up going with one whom she recommended for me. Being that both designers had a wonderful rapport, it made it very easy for me. This meant one would pick up right where the other left off in terms of understanding design. I didn't have to try to convey to the layout designer what the cover designer had done. That saved me lots of time.

Working with two significant experts in the field gave me tremendous confidence and peace of mind. It freed me up to do other things while they communicated and created a beautifully designed book.

It is noteworthy to mention that it was the work of these two phenomenal designers that enhanced my work, which led me to being published by a traditional house in New York. The cover design and feel of the book sold it!

The Specialists You Need on Your Team

1. Book Cover Designer
2. Book Interior Designer
3. Book Copy Writer for Back Cover
4. Book Editor and Proofreader
5. Professional Photographer specializing in head shots
6. Web Designer-specializing in working with authors

7. 2-5 Book Readers and Reviewers
8. Social Media Expert who specializes in working with authors

If you are working with a professional book writing and marketing coach, that person should already have these individuals in place for you. Personally, I like to align individuals on my team that best suit the needs and personality of the client. I have a variety of professional people I can go to for almost any need a client may have at any given moment.

One of the things I set as a priority with my book writers is the importance of building a budget for the project. The value of having a budget with a timeline is vital. It is taken into consideration as part of the plan for growing their business and covering their expenses. Knowing their financial goals also helps me better serve them. I make it a point to connect them with a team that is going to best match their budgetary needs. The idea is to make it easy and accelerate the whole process for them.

Tips for Building Your Publishing Support Team

I'd like to speak to some of the things that writers and authors can easily miss when hiring specialists. It is easy to think that an editor is an editor or a web designer is a web designer. What do I mean by that? Unless one knows to look for certain distinctions, it is easy to miss some of the important aspects of working with these experts. This is why getting clear on what you want makes it easy to find.

If you are a writer who likes to write as you speak, you may want to work with an editor who is a little more relaxed over someone who is more likely to be too rigid. Choosing the right editor is critical because the wrong editor may change the voice of the writer or author. There is a fine line between the old adage, *going by the book*, and changing the expression of one's words.

Also, it is important to mention that there are different types of editors depending on the scope of work. In most cases, I refer to copy editors and proofreaders. Since I incorporate the developmental side of editing within my services, my clients don't have the need for a development editor. However, this type of editor handles more of the content or story flow.

In any case, the best thing to do is to ask the editors to edit two to three pages of your writing in order to sample their work. Many writers make the mistake of handing over the whole manuscript only to find their work has been completely red-rivered with markings. Offering two or three editors a few pages at the same time will give you an opportunity to compare who is the best match for you.

In addition, if you are choosing an editor

yourself, make sure to tell them what you want! Don't settle for anything less than what you want in terms of making sure that your thoughts and words are not compromised in any way.

In the event you are not working with a professional book writing coach, chances are you or your assistant will be managing each of the individuals who touch your project.

Before hiring anyone, it is recommended to have a signed agreement with them that covers the *scope of work*: the expectations based on deadlines, delivery of services or products, and the rights to the work. At the risk of sounding like a broken record, please protect your intellectual rights.

In terms of timing, in many cases the editor can be working on the interior while the cover designer is working on the cover. This will free you up to focus on the design, look and feel of your book. One should strive to be complete with the front and back cover design before the editing is complete.

You can then focus on the edits and going through the whole book line by line to make sure everything is perfect. Ideally your interior layout designer will be standing by, waiting for you to be done with your edits.

Once the layout is complete, then you can upload the polished version with both covers and spine to a POD company that will take a lot of the worry and trouble out of publishing, distribution and fulfillment (e.g. CreateSpace).

Another area that requires some illumination for authors is web design. If you're just starting out, three to five pages (or just a link that takes you to a quick introduction of you and your book) will work well. The key is to keep it simple.

While working with designers, know whether you are the type of person that wants to be able to make changes or would rather have someone else do it for you. If you like doing things yourself, then you want to find a designer that can offer you patience while you learn as well as an easy approach. This will require less time compared to the time required of being enrolled in a class.

We want to be on the lookout for things and people that encourage us to work smart. In doing so, we can utilize our time far more efficiently! Working with someone who makes it easy to learn and get where you need to get quickly is definitely somebody worth paying! I look for professionals who love what they do, simply because it makes the learning curve less of an experiment.

Knowing how you like to learn and communicate will help you identify the web designer who is just the right person to teach you. For example, whether you like to learn visually or audibly may be important for your designer to know! It will save you and your designer lots of time, which may allow you to be able to accomplish more by phone or Skype. If you like to learn with the person in front of you, then you will need to express that as well.

Five Ways eBooks can Grow Your Business

Although I can easily write a whole book on the value of eBooks, my intent is to keep things simple and concise for you. As you will see, there is a variety of creative marketing strategies that an author can take with an eBook. This is an extraordinary way to publish your material.

1. One of the most simple and effective things to do is to take several of your chapters and offer them as individual eBooks. This is why planning your chapter headings before writing your book can make it easy for you to give so much more to your audience. There are three main reasons for taking the approach of using your chapters as eBooks:

   The first reason is that it allows you to potentially reach a much larger scope of people within your target market. For example, I can take any one of my chapters and sell each as a separate unit to reach writers and authors who have different needs and are in different stages of writing.

The second reason is that it allows you to also test your market and potentially grow your business by offering teleseminars and webinars on each angle you explore. You can also offer the eBook that goes with the event as a bonus.

The third reason is you can price each eBook accordingly, which is typically less than you would charge for your entire book. This also gives you an opportunity to potentially make more money with, for instance, three or four eBooks (depending on prices) for about the same price you might list the original book. So, you could double your sales by selling eBooks along with your original book. You can also give an eBook away as a lead-in to several other products you may have available on your website for purchase.

2. With an eBook, you can include links to direct your audience to your site, to a joint venture partner's site, and Youtube videos—just to name a few. Another benefit to creating a series of eBooks is using them as a free opt-in to build your database on your website. You can sell your book as well as other products with an eBook.

3. You can offer one or more of your eBooks as a complimentary giveaway or create a campaign with a joint venture partner, especially

if you make it to benefit their audience in a big way!

You can also make eBooks out of the subcategories within your book as opposed to using chapters. For instance, there are several headers within this chapter. I can easily make the subcategory header to this very section into an eBook entitled *Five Ways eBooks can Grow Your Business*. The same can be done with one of my other subcategories, *The Ten Most Common Marketing Mistakes Made by Writers and Authors.* In fact, to show you how limitless we can be with the creative process of marketing, an eBook for several of the individual mistakes can also be developed as well!

Can you see how beneficial it would be to either include eBooks as part of the content for blogs or as part of social media campaigns that lead to introducing events? My examples of the material contained within these pages are used primarily to show you what it looks like to expand your material into other products.

4. Another suggestion is to use one or more eBooks to create a home study program simply by adding specific exercises, quizzes, lessons, etc.

The main point to remember is that eBooks can be used primarily as an introduction to your *bigger* work such as your teleseminars, training sessions, coaching, live events, etc. I see them as mini commercials or representations of the scope of knowledge you can offer the people within your market.

People sometimes get caught up on the length of their eBooks. My suggestion once again is the same as it is for regular books. It is not the number of pages that should concern one but the quality of information being offered within those pages. That said, I will attempt to offer some suggestions. Though there is some variance of opinion, I feel the length should be determined by the purpose behind using an eBook.

For example, if you're using an eBook as a tool that will introduce people to a training program or workshop you're offering, you probably want to offer the major highlights that will be included. Thirty to fifty pages would be more than ample to whet appetites and create curiosity. I could take the chapter "Get Paid While You Write Your Book" and offer it as an expanded version in an eBook. This eBook would be used as a tool for inviting people to a workshop, seminar or online event. I would then tailor the information to specifically address the needs of the individuals who attend the event.

Keeping benefits always in the forefront, I would create it so that each person who attends the event will walk away with three very specific strategies.

Each of the attendees will also have the option of working with me or one of my coaches to further implement those strategies with our accelerated coaching program.

I offer this example as a way to show you the progression that can easily take place with the initial idea of using an eBook as a tool. The quality offered within those few pages need to really speak to the needs of your audience. The eBook needs to be proportional on a much smaller scale to the amplification of value offered at the live event. In other words, there needs to be the same high level of quality and information shared in both. The only difference is that one is live, allowing you to really play with your audience and give them more advice.

The Copyright Page

The purpose of a copyright page is to establish the rights of the author as it pertains to intellectual property. Since the copyright page is usually placed on the back side of the title page, it is one of the first things people will see when they open a book. This page should be very polished, and highlight each listed element separately in regards to its own importance. The font size is typically smaller than that used for the content.

All excerpts from books written by other authors will require you to obtain a release from the author and/

or the publishing company before publishing your book. This is very critical as acknowledging these titles, authors, publishers and copyright year of publication is essential on the copyright page. It is here that gratitude for permission to reprint previously published materials is offered.

Any disclaimers and/or intentions on behalf of the author are also to be treated as a separate element. This particular element allows for the author to disclaim any and all responsibilities to the reader.

The Ten Main Elements of A Copyright Page

Regardless of genre or type of book, when it comes to publishing there are some things that are considered as part of the industry standard. Here's a list of items that will guide you to accentuate your copyright page.

1. A simple line such as "Grateful acknowledgement is made to the following for permission to reprint previously published material:" will suffice as you can list all of the information below this line.

2. Although there are many variations of order in placement, there are other specific elements that are to be included on this page on the same line: the word "Copyright" with the symbol ©, the year it is being printed, and your name as the author.

3. The next item is the paragraph that speaks to your intellectual rights and usually begins with "All rights reserved".

4. The name of the publisher

5. Where it is being printed (e.g. Printed in The United States of America)

6. "Design by" followed by the cover and book interior designers along with "Illustrated by" below as a separate line

7. Library of Congress-Cataloging-in-Publication Data-(referring to your book categories)

8. Your name as the author followed by the number of edition

9. ISBN and number

10. The number of edition

When it comes to the ins and outs of copyright law, however, I defer to my client and dear friend, Maria Crimi Speth: a licensed attorney and author of *Protect Your Writings*, the first of her series of copyright books. I am so grateful that Maria wrote this book because it covers the main area of law protecting the written word and how to avoid costly legal mistakes. As I learned in working with her, there is so much for writers and authors to learn in this area.

What I really enjoyed about working with Maria was how passionate she is, in addition to her willingness to help others. One of the stories I love to tell about her speaks directly to her discipline in getting her book written in a rather short time.

She decided to take an hour a week to write her book given her busy schedule as an attorney, wife, mother, author, and speaker. So with that intention in mind, she sat down every Sunday and wrote a chapter or pretty close to a complete chapter. She would then send her writing to me to review for our call on the next Monday. By the end of our call, we would create the goal of what she would write the following Sunday.

Not everyone feels they can do a chapter in an hour, but Maria's story reminds me of what is possible when we know what we want in life. I was so impressed with her determination because she never wavered from her focus to complete her work. I find so much joy in working with individuals who love what they do and do it extraordinarily!

"It's not how many things we master but how many things we do masterfully!"

– Stella Togo

CHAPTER 7

MASTERFUL MARKETING & THE TOP 15 STREAMS OF INCOME

When I think back to my fear of reaching *high* notes in singing, I remember how easy it would have been to stop myself from going any further. I was so petrified just at the thought of making a complete fool of myself in front of an audience. This was new territory for me. There were so many unknowns. The only thing I knew was I was scared to death!

Since my definition of high notes was associated with fear, Betty showed me I needed to completely redefine this aspect. I didn't even think that was possible. I soon realized that having fear about something just meant I needed more information.

In class, she started to train us to turn our bodies side to side every time we sang a high note. At first this seems like one of those exercises where you rub your belly and the top of your head at the same time. It felt awkward and silly to me. Strangely, the more we did it, the more comfortable it became to reach those notes.

What was interesting was that I stopped thinking about the notes, because I had to concentrate on the movement. Another benefit to moving was that it seemed to relax my body as well as my vocal chords.

Betty went a step further and told us to drive to where we could see a freeway moving from both directions. I managed to find the perfect location near my gym.

As I drove up, I noticed a parked car with an African American man sleeping in the front seat with a fedora hat over his face. I parked so I could have my perfect view while creating enough distance between our cars. The sound of the freeway was rather loud, but I cracked the front windows for some air circulation. As I intensely watched the cars fly by in front of me, I reached notes I didn't think I would ever find within my range.

I was so lost in my music that I totally forgot about my surroundings. At one point, I looked up from my sheet music and to my right. There I saw one of the sweetest smiles I'd ever seen on the face of the elderly man sitting in his car. He motioned for me to roll down my passenger side window so I did, curious as to what he was going to say to me. To my utter astonishment, he started asking me questions as to how long I had been singing! I couldn't believe he could hear me between the freeway noise and the fact that my window was only slightly cracked! Once I realized he heard me, I wondered if I had awakened him. He assured me I had not and expressed that he thoroughly enjoyed listening to me. He further went on to say that it had been a special treat. I'll never forget him and his kind words.

The more I embraced the association of *the side to side* with my high notes, the more I felt freed up to sing them! Being more at ease allowed me to linger much longer on those notes. I began to feel more confident, and I was able to release my fear. When I think about it, it was just a simple adjustment and a new way of thinking that completely changed everything for me. Oh, My Dear Betty! How I miss you!

Though I don't claim to have mastered my opera singing like the great high sopranos of the world, I was trained to sing masterfully.

I feel that many authors have a lot of fear around many, if not all aspects of marketing and sales. Generally speaking there is fear of rejection and the sense that one has to be a really great sales-person in order to be a successful authorpreneur. The mere idea of having to convince people to buy their books keeps potential authors stuck. It is that same idea that holds them hostage within their own minds.

For many writers it would be much easier to focus on writing because the fear of marketing runs so deep—they'd rather not think about it. But what if there was another way of looking at marketing? What if there is another *side to side* association that could give you a different definition? What if it wasn't really about selling at all?

You might think I have lost my mind! What if you started looking at ways you could truly help the people in your market? What if you knew that associating them with having to make sales was completely an injustice to them?

The fact of the matter is that masterful marketing is all about getting intimately engaged with the needs of the people who make up your markets. The association in this case is as simple as the *side to side* association with my high notes.

Here's another example to explain it further... I experienced how the Nordstrom family's focus on helping people find great shoes and providing extraordinary customer service revolutionized the retail industry. As employees, offering the very best quality of service and merchandise was always first and foremost on our minds.

Clients whom I serviced were like family to me. I

knew their birthdays, anniversaries, as well as what they loved and wanted at all times. In fact, we were the ones they called when they made their travel plans to help them with their clothing needs. Our training in providing outstanding services made it easy to wholeheartedly care about our customers. Sales followed naturally because we sincerely earned their trust.

It wasn't about talking someone into buying something at all because the merchandise could easily be returned. It was about finding what customers needed for their next special event and calling them up unexpectedly to say we had found some beautiful items. The employees who typically didn't make it were the ones who primarily focused on reaching their quotas without great service.

Working the long hours didn't matter as long as we knew we did our very best to take care of every customer who came into shop that day. We may not have been masters at our young age as many of us were barely in our twenties, yet we were trained to sell masterfully. We were well compensated for giving the gift of providing incomparable customer service and merchandise.

What is Your Gift?

What outstanding gift can you provide your customers, clients and readers to fulfill their needs? The more you can focus on fulfilling their needs with that gift, the faster and easier your business will grow!

1. Is your gift in speaking?

2. Is your gift providing great service, and in what capacity?

3. Is your gift in teaching so people can learn easily?

4. Is your gift in being an outstanding listener?

5. Is your gift in technology?

6. Is your gift in the visual arts?

7. Is your gift in the performing arts?

8. Is your gift in writing and expressing yourself with the written word?

The more gifts you can be aware of, the more you can use them to reach your target market. So often people try to do what everyone else is doing instead of what comes natural to them. It's important to separate your gifts from your skillset for the moment. There's a distinction between the two that is often overlooked in sales and marketing.

Anyone can be trained to do almost anything they're passionate about; things that come the easiest to an individual are in many cases the very things that merit far more attention. In fact, it may be very beneficial to list your gifts as part of your new association with marketing. The key is to ask yourself what could you tirelessly do all day long? Identifying that one thing that brings you the most joy will take the hard work out of your marketing!

For example, if your gift lies in speaking well and having great communication skills, you might really enjoy creating an audio version of your book as an additional product. You may enjoy learning more about blog radio talk shows as well as get excited about interviewing guests on your topic. You might enjoy doing a teleseminar, not to mention a variety of speaking events.

If your gift is being an outstanding listener, you might really enjoy mentoring with your expertise people within your market. Depending on the demographics of your market, you may want to create a series of mentoring programs for different age groups.

It is essential to start with your gifts first. It then gets a lot easier to add your skillset in order to expand your possibilities. This is where it gets really exciting in working with my clients. When you establish a way to use your gifts coupled with your skills to fulfill a specific need, there is only one more thing to do!

Yes, the only thing that's left is to choose which

streams of revenue best suit your gifts and skillset. Though the possibilities are beyond measure, I believe it is best to go with what brings you the greatest joy and opportunities. Given the title of this chapter, I am fulfilling the promise of offering you the list of the top fifteen streams of income.

The Top 15 Streams of Income for Writers and Authors

1. Your Book and/or Series of Books
2. eBooks
3. Training
4. Workshops
5. Seminars
6. Publicity
7. Video
8. Home Study Programs and Products
9. Joint Venturing/Affiliate Programs/Authors/ Experts
10. Talk Radio, Blog Talk Radio, Audio
11. Speaking
12. Live Events

13. Teleseminars

14. Webinars

15. Mentoring/Coaching

Being a published author certainly offers a great deal of credibility and visibility. Your book is your new business card which opens the doors to tremendous opportunities. As you can see, there are many ways to create revenue and many authors will choose several of the listed streams.

The key to remember is that starting with a book with *the million dollar seed approach* promotes building each activity and product onto the other. This also works well when you start with offering workshops, webinars or teleseminars as you write your book.

Your Built-in Stream of Income Strategy

Establishing your book as the seed of your business, gives you the actual foundation to build it as big as your heart desires! It is a very methodical way of growing your revenue as your chapters and subheadings are intentionally designed with this larger picture in mind. This allows you to take any or all of your chapter titles or subheadings and use them as topics to speak on, teach, mentor, write about… etc.

You may need to tweak a word or two or consider combining a few headings together at times for different streams, but you get the gist. For instance, I may replace the word *seed* with *book* or combine a couple of subheadings within my chapter on self-publishing for a teleseminar or workshop. However, the possibilities are endless. The alignment that occurs across the board with branding and clarity is truly profound for you and your audience.

A good guideline is to have a minimum of twenty-five angles or topic titles based on your content for a self-help or how-to book. Can you imagine the range of built-in choices with this guideline? It's all very mathematical in essence. For example, an author can select three points they intend to speak to for each of their ten chapters. That would give them thirty subcategories—plus the ten chapter titles!

Although there are variations with different types of books such as novels and children's books, the approach is the same. This foundation of information allows an author to systematically choose the stream or streams of revenue that best fits their gifts.

Your book as the seed makes it fun, exciting and easy to develop a business plan complete with timelines and revenue goals. This is why an expert author today can call what they want to earn and make a lot of money. Herein is positioned the new paradigm for being a successful authorpreneur.

Design Your Templates for Your Products

When it comes to creating products, they too can be designed to follow these headings for your talks, home study programs, trainings, and coaching packages. The most efficient way to create new products is to start with a template or specific design for the content. With a template in mind, you won't need to start from scratch every time as it offers a well-established built-in plan.

I like to think of templates as the structure to the information or content of any product or stream of income. For instance, one can create a template for a speaking engagement for flow and desired outcome. The topic may change but the format is set for every talk thereafter. There is so much to share when it comes to making sure that every aspect or component needed is covered for your audience. This goes for every template designed for it needs to meet the needs of your target.

Having a template in place for a book series makes it so easy to simply fill in the blanks. I can't begin to tell you how much time is saved and the confidence gained just from the peace of mind. The profound sense of organization that is obtained is insurmountable!

Another great benefit to designing a template is it helps you test different markets faster. You can take the same format even with an email blast. And if creating templates doesn't speak to your gifts, hire someone who can design them for you! All that is needed is what's important to your people within your market. Humor is also a great component that makes any type of template fun to develop.

Social Media Channels

It took me a while before I was able to completely grasp the whole idea of social media. Initially I saw it as a true waste of time. I simply didn't understand why people felt the need to share photos of their dinners. It wasn't until I was able to see the real significance behind this tool that I began to understand its purpose.

The greatest beauty about social media is the endless opportunities to connect with other like-minded people. Since building relationships is key to reaching a lot of your target market, having a strategy is highly recommended for writers and authors.

If a writer can launch conversations regarding their topics prior to publishing, this will give them a leg up on building important relationships. Using the book's chapter titles and subheadings will help them blog and test the market for response. This is one of the most effective ways to connect and create interest in your topic. Your book will be well received by a captive audience.

There is a lot to say about social media and internet marketing and quite frankly, that would take another book. However, I earnestly believe in it and encourage you to make the connections that will take you to the next level.

I see it as a great way to make a contribution by supporting the efforts of other professionals. Connecting with group, company and organization leaders is key for the growth of all of our businesses; especially when we are catering to the same audience. Also, joining efforts with magazines and their chief editors can also be very beneficial for authors.

Editors need great information for their audiences and may be interested in interviewing you. They may even ask for an excerpt from your book. It's always a good idea to do your homework first to see how you may be of support to them. Study their publication closely before contacting them. Your preparation time will give you vital information and confidence. Remember it is about serving and supporting them.

Masterful marketing begins with you, your gifts and skills to support a specific group of people known as your market. Connect and get to know them so well that your books and products will sell themselves. Share your gifts and experience a new world!

"Knowing where we come from helps us better understand and appreciate where we are"

– Stella Togo

IN CLOSING

A NOTE FROM STELLA

When I think of planting seeds and gardening, I fondly remember my father coming inside with baskets full of zucchini that looked like they had been injected with hormones! I was always surprised by how their juice would spurt as I sliced them. My mother would then take them along with the zucchini flowers and cook up the most delicious Italian frittata. Bless his heart—Papà could grow most anything as he had the most amazing green thumb.

He proudly showed me his garden every time I'd visit my parents at their home. I was always taken by the conscious love he poured into each plant and fruit tree. The delicious results of his harvest were truly a true testament to his passion for his gardening.

I find it rather serendipitous that *The Million Dollar Seed* became the title to this work, because

I come from more generations than I can count of farmers in Italy. For many centuries, my ancestors cultivated acres of land filled with olive and almond trees. I am the first of my generation born here in the United States as well as the first author and entrepreneur.

My father always spoke of how he came to America so that his children could live the American dream. It was important to him and my mother to instill in us the importance of using our heads instead of working with our hands while earning a good living. I feel their beliefs resulted from seeing their parents and grandparents labor in the fields.

I am very grateful for the way this body of work has come to fruition—funny how that word is so appropriate! I have lipstick on my ears from smiling so big!

The amazing thing about writing is that it typically takes on a life of its own. Like many writers and authors, I feel I am definitely a conduit. The material seemed to have poured right through me. In fact, there were moments where I had to ice my hands because I was typing so much in such a short time! I thoroughly enjoyed the process and knew nothing could stop me from reaching my goal.

Herein is expressed my truth, experiences and personal accounts all for the purpose of making it easier for other writers and authors. *You* are the reason I share this content. I have written it in hopes that you will have a greater sense of peace of mind, given my offerings of strategies and short cuts. I am so thankful for the opportunity to share it with you.

In the world of writing and marketing, so many people feel alone. It is my intention for you to feel embraced with this work and to know you are cared for. Though I may not know you personally, I have shared your frustrations and rejections in the past. However, today is a new day! Today I share your successes and celebrate your accomplishments.

Like my father who poured his love into growing his garden, I have poured my love into *this* seed for you. May your writing and business growth be greatly accelerated with profound clarity and intention for the benefit of your readers and audiences.

I hope you will stop by and visit me at my site www.stellatogo.com from time to time just to say hello or to let me know what is working for you as a result of this content. I'd love to hear about your success. I look forward to connecting with you soon!

With Love and Appreciation,

Stella Togo

NOTES

Notes

Notes

Notes

Notes

Notes

Notes

Notes

Notes

Notes

Made in the USA
Charleston, SC
04 October 2013